Meet the Psychics and Read Their Incredible Stories!

"The first time I read for Yoko Ono, I had a vision of John Lennon. I could see blood coming out of his body. I told her, 'He sleeps in blood.' She asked what that meant, and I said, 'It's not a happy ending.'" (p. 4)

"A screenwriter came to me for a reading and I told him, 'The way to your success is going to be through novel writing, and through the novel you'll write your screenplay.' He wound up writing a 'record-breaking novel.' And *then* he received an offer to write the screenplay. Now he's a multimillionaire." (p. 211)

"I read for a woman whose boyfriend worked for the CIA and I elaborated on many of his activities. The woman recorded the reading and played the tape for him. He was startled at its accuracy and wanted her to destroy the tape to protect his private missions." (p. 257)

"I told a woman who had a yellow Volkswagen to be real careful the first week of December because I saw her having an accident. She said, 'It's my vacation time so I'll stay home.' She took care of her grandson, who had a little toy Volkswagen on the kitchen floor, and she stepped on it and broke her leg." (p. 269)

Books by Paulette Cooper and Paul Noble

Reward!*
The 100 Top Psychics in America*
277 Secrets Your Dog Wants You to Know

Other Books by Paulette Cooper

The Scandal of Scientology
The Medical Detectives

*Published by POCKET BOOKS

THE
100
TOP
PSYCHICS

IN AMERICA

THEIR STORIES, SPECIALTIES— AND HOW TO CONTACT THEM

PAULETTE COOPER
AND PAUL NOBLE

POCKET BOOKS
New York   London   Toronto   Sydney   Tokyo   Singapore

Ouija is a registered trademark for Parker Brothers.

An *Original* Publication of POCKET BOOKS

POCKET BOOKS, a division of Simon & Schuster Inc.
1230 Avenue of the Americas, New York, NY 10020

ISBN: 0-671-53401-7

First Pocket Books printing September 1996

10 9 8 7 6 5 4 3 2 1

POCKET and colophon are registered trademarks of Simon & Schuster Inc.

Cover design by Brigid Pearson

Printed in the U.S.A.

This book is dedicated to

*the children of the future
and our nieces and nephews
who are part of it:*

*Chaim, Danielle, Jacob,
Orly, Itamar, Rachel, Sarah*

Contents

Introduction

You are about to read the personal stories of America's top psychics. Some of these individuals are famous; some have channeled the famous, and some have read for the famous. Their clients have included John Lennon, Yoko Ono, Marilyn Monroe, Jerry Garcia, Grace Kelly, Howard Hughes, Madonna, Elvis Presley, John Wayne, River Phoenix, Tony Curtis, Mick Jagger, Kim Basinger—and people just like you.

Those featured here include love psychics, crime psychics, business psychics, general psychics, animal psychics, and psychic astrologers; a lottery psychic, an Oscar psychic, a car psychic, a location psychic, a mining psychic, and an earthquake psychic; psychics who read tarot, tea leaves, auras, and candles; channelers, mediums, and healers; and those who help people with life options, business options, or stock options.

This is the first inside look ever at this mysterious group. Until now, the majority of psychics have operated without most people, including their own clients, knowing exactly what they do. And why. We decided to present their stories in their own words, with only light editing, so you would have the chance to learn *who* these people are and how they got where they are.

We have also included how you can contact them either by phone or by mail. Some didn't want to have their addresses printed, others, their phone numbers, which is why there aren't both addresses and phone numbers for everyone. But they can be reached in some way, and we tell you how to do it.

Most of the psychics included in this book are available for personal (and often for phone) readings. Surprisingly, a sixty-minute reading with most of them—even the most established—usually costs less than the same amount of time with a "hot line" psychic.

The way these psychics were chosen was as follows. First, they had to be recommended by their peers, by the media, by their clients, by psychic researchers, or by psychic organizations that we contacted. (Often, they were recommended by at least two of these sources.)

Then they had to pass the first hurdle: our cynicism. We read over a thousand articles written about those who were suggested, and we watched and listened to hundreds of videotapes and audiotapes of shows they had been on.

Those who remained were then pre-interviewed at great length by one of our two researchers—one of whom once hosted a New Age radio show, and the other of whom published a New Age magazine. After we went through the transcripts of these interviews, we personally interviewed those psychics we believed qualified to be among the top psychics in America.

Our final step was to run those names past several psychics, not to find out what they could "see" about them but rather what they *knew* about them. We thought it important that only those highly thought of by their peers be included in this book.

Those who survived this rigorous selection process are included here. The majority of those who were initially recommended for this book are not.

Most of the psychics are presented in full interview, but some are simply mentioned, with only their specialty and a contact number. A few of these people did not want to be interviewed in depth; several were traveling at the time we wrote the book or were located too late to allow for a full interview.

Some well-known psychics weren't included in this book. This doesn't necessarily mean that they're not at the same level as those who are here. We had to make a few personal decisions about whom to exclude: several psychics elicited a negative response from their peers; some we were never able to locate; others didn't want publicity; and a couple may have been missed through human error. We are planning to update this book, so we may get to some of them the next time.

We also want to add that we take no legal or moral responsibility for leaving anyone out or for putting anyone in. If you write or call any of these people and are unhappy with the results, bear in mind that we did not recommend any of them. We just told you who appeared to be the top in a field few people know much about.

It is also possible that addresses or phone numbers may have changed after we went to press. If you want to reach someone and can't, send them a letter through us at the address below, and we'll try to forward your letter.

Because we expect that this book will be updated, we invite your input. If you wish to nominate new people or have any experiences with those in this book that you'd like to share with us, please write.

Finally, we'd like to thank all of those people and organizations who helped us choose the psychics in this book. We also thank Mary Houston who helped to locate and preinterview some of them. We especially wish to thank our new friend Marille Fendelman, who took part in every aspect of this book: locating people; interviewing them; writing up early drafts; and helping us put it all together.

We thank our agent, Ted Chichak, for twenty years of loyalty and good advice. We're very pleased to be working once again under Bill Grose and especially happy to be with our favorite editor, Molly Allen, whose skills and good advice are matched only by her wit and cheerful personality.

Paulette Cooper and Paul Noble
Post Office Box 20541
Cherokee Station
New York, New York 10021
or PauletteC@aol.com
or PaulRnoble@aol.com

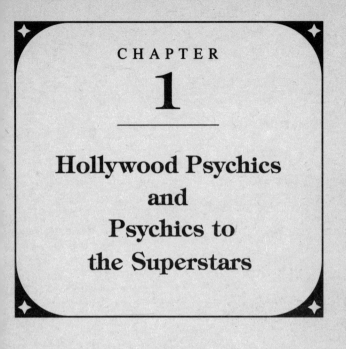

CHAPTER
1

Hollywood Psychics
and
Psychics to
the Superstars

FRANK ANDREWS

261 MULBERRY STREET
NEW YORK, NEW YORK 10012
(212) 226-2194
E-mail: FANDRYNYC@aol.com

Photo by Tim Dalal © 1995

He is sometimes called the "Rolls-Royce of psychics" because he has read for John Lennon, Yoko Ono, Grace Kelly, Christina Ford, and Perry Ellis, among others.

Did you and John Lennon hit it off? We did and we didn't. See, if they don't like what I have to say, they get very upset. They want to hear that it's all going to be wonderful and everything is going to be roses. I don't blame them, but I can't do that unless that's the way it is. So what I try to do is find a way to make it wonderful and to make it roses.

What kind of questions did John ask? During my first reading with John, in his kitchen at the Dakota, every time I would tell him the truth, he would say, "You read that somewhere."

Still, he kept asking me questions like "Will the Beatles get together again?" "No," I told him, "but I see them on Broadway." Of course, we later had *Beatlemania.*

I also suggested to John that he was troubled by his homosexuality. "Why do you dress Yoko up as a boy?" I asked him. He was furious. I also read his palm and found signs of conflict and madness.

How did you end up as Yoko's reader? Although John was a little upset about some of the things I had to say, he told me once that I was very clever.

But after I had been reading him mostly, he said, "You know everyone wants to know me. Why don't you know Yoko? She's the one who needs a friend. Why don't you be Yoko's friend." So I worked with her for about ten years.

Did you foresee John's murder? The first time I read for Yoko, when I was just about finished, I had a vision of John. I immediately felt that there was something wrong. I could see blood coming out of his body. I told her, "He sleeps in blood." She asked what that meant, and I said, "It's not a happy ending."

What about your experience with Princess Grace? The first time I read for her I said, "Would you like to hear this as the princess or as Grace?" She smiled and kissed me on the cheek and said, "Honey, tell me like it is!" So I just went to town and let her have it.

What was the most significant thing you told her? That she should leave her husband, get out of Monaco, go back to Hollywood, and start acting again. The strange thing about one reading, though, was that she said, "There's one thing I have to ask you. Do you feel I'm going to die in a car?" "Why do say that?" I asked. "I have a premonition," she said.

She wanted me to come to Monaco, but I never saw her after that.

Did she tell people she had seen you? When she

was on *Entertainment Tonight,* she said she met the "famous psychic Frank Andrews." I thought that was so funny, her being who she was. And then she said, "He said I should go back to Hollywood and act." She had just started getting back into it when she died.

What happened with Andy Warhol? He actually did a painting of me, although he never had a reading by me because he was too frightened of what I might see for him.

After I got the portrait, we went to dinner, and I picked a card for him. I slid it across the table; it was the death card. That was the last time I saw him. He was dead three months later. He sort of knew. He felt it.

Have you worked with other famous people? Many. For example, when Perry Ellis came to me, he was in marketing; he wasn't a designer. And I saw him as a designer. But when I told him, he laughed at me and thought I was crazy.

Do you have clients who aren't famous? My clients include everyone from waiters to some of the world's richest people. I feel I can help almost anyone. For example, about twenty years ago, there was this guy I was reading for, and the whole reading was about him leaving his wife. I told him I didn't like the girlfriend he was going to run away with. His bags were packed, but I said to him, "Why don't you give it a month? If after that nothing changes, then you can leave." He said that his mind was made up, and I said, "No it isn't, because if it was, why did you come to see me?"

Did you ever learn what happened? Well, I didn't see him for fifteen years, and I wondered what happened to him. Then I saw him again. He said he had told his girlfriend that something came up and he couldn't leave for a couple of weeks. So she went and married somebody else! "How much could she have loved you if in two weeks she meets a guy and runs off?" I asked him. "God, did you pick them badly."

Do you wish some people wouldn't call you? I don't like when people become dependent on me. I don't like it when they call too much. When they don't call, I know they were able to figure it out. It's very rare that anyone calls and says, "Everything is great. Everything is wonderful." They usually call when there's a crisis.

Are there some things you don't like to do? I don't want people to call me to do séances anymore. I did them in the '80s. It's too much of a nuisance to get all the telephones repaired. The energy generated by the séances wrecked electrical fuses and ruined my telephones. The guy used to scream at me when I would bring the phones in for repair. "What do you do with these phones?" he'd ask me.

Do you feel you owe your technique to anyone else? My method is, I take a little bit of Carl Jung, Freud, Einstein, Alfred Adler, Christianity, Judaism, Zen Buddhism, and Islam, and I kind of mix it all up and I go with it.

How do you combine tarot and palmistry? I work with the tarot, palmistry, and hand analysis. Tarot tells you visually what's going on right now, and palmistry gives you an overall picture of what's going on along with character analysis and what kind of work the person is suited for.

How often do you see your clients? I don't like to see more than four people a day because it's very tiring. I ask them not to come more often than once a year. I'd rather read the cards for a stranger than someone I know, because if I know them, I'm colored and influenced by my own feelings.

Have you helped people with financial decisions? I have accurately predicted mergers, located oil-drilling sites, and picked stocks that have gone from 20 to 120.

I said to one very rich client, "Are you going to invest in Broadway?" And he said, "No, I hate shows. I wouldn't do that." I said, "That's funny. There's something here about a Broadway show. I think it's a musical. It looks pretty good!"

A few years later I saw him again, and he said to me, "Remember that musical you talked to me about? I invested in it." It turned out it was *Annie*. He had put in two million dollars—and got back twenty to one.

What was your first prediction? At one point, I was studying pantomime—that's what I really wanted to do in life—and I was studying in a dance class with Michael Bennett. I said to him, "You know, Michael, you're going to be

very, very famous one day. I can see you on Broadway."
Well, he became known as "Mr. Broadway" because he did
so many big musicals, like *A Chorus Line* and *Dream Girls*.
In fact, one of the characters in *A Chorus Line* was patterned
after me.

ARLENE DAHL

DAHLMARK PRODUCTIONS
POST OFFICE BOX 116
SPARKILL, NEW YORK 10976
FAX: (212) 956-7524

As psychic as she is beautiful, she has starred in thirty movies and nineteen plays and authored thirteen books on astrology and beauty.

What were your most dramatic psychic experiences? I had three out-of-body experiences. The first time, early in my career in Hollywood, I was in a terrible automobile accident. The convertible I was in turned over twice—and we didn't have seat belts then. I was unconscious, doctors couldn't find a pulse, and I didn't appear to be breathing.

What do you recall of this? The doctors were examining me on the table in the emergency ward, and I saw and felt myself floating below the ceiling, looking down at myself on the table and at what they were doing. When I came to—

and back into my body—I was in intensive care. I felt very light-headed, remembered what had happened, and told the doctor where he had been standing, how everyone had been positioned around me, and the conversations that went on.

What about the other times? The second time was a horseback riding accident, and the third time was during my son Lorenzo's birth, in which we both almost lost our lives.

When did you get into tea leaf reading? After my long recovery period from the auto accident, I was invited to a weekend party. I went to a Beverly Hills bookstore and found a book called *Tea Leaf Reading at a Glance*. To amuse the guests, I brought along some gold earrings, an off-the-shoulder blouse, and a colorful Gypsy skirt. When the host served tea, I came out in my Gypsy outfit, lit some candles, and started reading the symbols.

Did you stick to the book or develop your own interpretations? Each time I looked at the book I felt that I was losing my audience, so I put the book aside and read what I saw of my own interpretations. The more I trusted my own intuition, the more on target I was.

Do you remember any of your successful readings that night? I told one gentleman, who I later discovered was the head of CBS, that he would have a success the following spring with a little girl who had the initial E next to her curly head. He was shocked, because the television series *Eloise* had just been signed for production that morning to begin the following spring. He confessed, "No one here knows about that, not even my wife!"

Did you continue your forecasts? No, I decided to drop it because I became frightened at my own accuracy! Six months later, however, I was making a film in London where they served tea twice a day. I started reading tea leaves again, and by the end of the film, I had read everyone's leaves. I went back to tea leaf reading because I realized that through this medium I could help people.

How did you learn about astrology? I had been in Hollywood just two weeks and was invited to the home of Hal Wallis's sister. A man came over to me and said, "Hello, Leo." I said, "My name is Arlene." He said, "But you were born in August, weren't you?" That man was Carroll Righter, the dean of American astrologers. Every star in those days had readings with him, including Marlene Dietrich, Ronald Reagan, and Jane Wyman. I attended his classes; he became my guru, and he wrote the introductions to my thirteen astrology books.

What were these books about? In 1950 I was the first to combine astrology with beauty and fashion in a syndicated beauty column. Simon & Schuster then asked me to write twelve astrology books about beauty, one for each sign of the zodiac, and my Beautyscope books sold over three million each. Then I wrote a book on astrological relationships, called *Lovescopes,* which became a popular cable television series.

Where does your psychic ability come in? I was not very good at numbers, but I excelled at the psychic interpretation of the charts. Now, thanks to the miracle of pocket calculators, I read charts for my friends and give them a psychic interpretation as well. I also read vibrations from tea leaves and tarot cards.

Do you always tell people what you see? I was taught by Carroll Righter not to be an alarmist. If someone asked me about a trip they were about to take and I felt that the plane may have engine trouble, I would try to persuade them to put off the flight, explaining it would be better timed and more successful if they went later.

Do you use your intuitive gifts with your husband? Yes, in fact, when I met my husband, Marc Rosen, at a business meeting, I went up to him and said, "Hello, Libra." He was stunned. I said, "I'll bet you were born around the end of September, around the twenty-ninth or thirtieth." He turned white and said, "Yes, the thirtieth." We became instant friends.

He is a famous package designer and recently won his fourth Fifi designer award for Halston's men's fragrance. With a full moon in Sag coming up and with Sag in his second house of money, coinciding with his moon, I knew there was a very good chance he would win.

Did you make predictions for your former husband, Fernando Lamas? Often. He was always rather skeptical until I told him that a musical he was up for with Ethel Merman in New York would bring him much success and Broadway accolades. Of course it did.

How have your forecasts helped your son, Lorenzo Lamas? He wanted a part in a new TV series written by Stephen Cannell. When he didn't get it, he called me, and I told him to go out and celebrate because something even better would come to him the following week. Ten days later he was offered the lead in the new series *Renegade,* produced by Stephen Cannell.

Did you use your psychic abilities when you were making movies? Yes, for example, I read Blake Edwards's tea leaves and told him, "You're going to make a comedy next year, and the star's initials are ES!" Blake said, "You're right. I'm directing *A Shot in the Dark* next spring, and you've got the *S* right for Sophia, but it should be *L* for Loren. She's agreed to star in it." But Sophia Loren dropped out of the film and was replaced by Elke Sommer!

JOHN GREEN

THE JOHN GREEN PSYCHIC CENTER
800 SUNSET BOULEVARD
LOS ANGELES, CALIFORNIA 90046
(818) 761-1114

Michael Preston, Photography

*This celebrity tarot reader has worked
with many famous people, and he wrote
up his experiences with John Lennon
and Yoko Ono in his book* Dakota Days.

When was your first meeting with the Lennons?
In the spring of 1974, when Frank Andrews was phasing out,
I got a call from someone who didn't give me her name but
said I was recommended by an actress friend of hers who
was my client. "I want a reading. You must come right
away," she whispered. She sounded like an elderly sick
woman, so I was pretty shocked when it was Yoko Ono who
opened the door.

What was she interested in? She was separated from
John at the time and wanted to get back with him. Over the

next several months I engineered that. Then I read for both of them, separately of course; John in the kitchen, and I'd read for her in the bedroom.

Did John want to know what you told Yoko? Actually, he would act as if he knew. "You've been telling Yoko about me again." Or, "You've been talking about ——— with her, haven't you?"

What did she want to get from a reading? She fancied herself as a psychic and used readers to double-check if she was right. She would also read to see if the psychics were right.

How did she do that? She'd ask the same questions of three different readers and then see which answers were most applicable to her life. If you can afford it, it's not a bad idea. It's like talking to more than one financial advisor.

Did it work for her? She had a tendency to look for the psychic who would reinforce what she wanted to hear versus what might be the most practical and correct answer. For example, sometimes she'd tell me, "I'm going to ask you about money. Don't tell me anything bad."

And what about John? Although songs had once poured out of him, he went for years without even writing a couplet and clearly was threatened by it. So his explorations in tarot were "Who am I?" and "What message can I send to my unconscious that will change this?"

What was he like personally? He was not an easy guy; talented, loving, funny, but at the same time an egomaniac, abusive to women. As an adolescent, he had been hailed as a genius and as a wit. He'd wave his fanny at the queen. Then he lost his ability to write music, and it devastated him.

What was their relationship like? An unending version of *Who's Afraid of Virginia Woolf?* It was often grim. The lighthearted, impish John was likely to be drunk and kicking her in the belly.

Did you help them in more ways than just personally? I read for them for seven years, until John's death. It was mostly on business, plus helping John get his green card and make some bizarre purchase. I also saved them over one hundred million dollars in lawsuits.

John was involved in thirteen lawsuits, and I was kept on twenty-four-hour call when cases were in trial to help them devise legal strategy. Twelve cases were won; one was settled.

Did you foresee John's death? He didn't ask about such things, but I did read that there was going to be a violent separation between the two of them. I anticipated that it would be marital, not murder.

Who were some of your other famous clients? I also read for Princess Yasmine Kahn, some of the Vanderbilts, DuPonts, and Fords. I met Jamie Lee Curtis, introduced myself, and told her I had once read for her father. She said, "Fine. Read for me." So I did. She's a very bright lady. Tony Curtis was a charming, humble, nice guy, a gentle, thoughtful fellow, who asked probing and interesting questions.

Were there any surprises in Tony Curtis's reading? For me, not for him. When I read for people, I always ask for their date of birth and their name as it appears on their birth certificate. I must have been the only person in the world who didn't know Tony Curtis's real name. So when I asked him his name and he said, "Bernie Schwartz," I thought maybe he was putting me on.

What did he want to know about? The same thing everyone asks about: love, money, and health. He also asked about business, because he was selecting roles in upcoming projects.

What was Mick Jagger like? I met him through John, and I expected all this wild hoopla and flamboyance. But he was a soft-spoken, very composed man who asked careful questions so as not to expose too much of himself and not to block out the information coming in. Among celebrity people, you don't usually meet that kind of careful, precise thinking.

Were your parents sympathetic to your psychic leanings? My father, who was a crane operator, was not. My mother's psychic roots go back three hundred years to one of her relatives who was a tarot reader and served as ship's surgeon for Captain Kidd.

When did you start reading for people, and what were their reactions? I started reading tarot cards part-time in college. The students were dazzled that I could describe what their fathers were like without meeting them. I became very popular as the big mystic on campus.

I worked my way through college as a psychic and also as a gravedigger, short-order cook, and salesman for the *New York Times*.

What did you do after college? I taught briefly and loathed it. Then I worked in publishing production. For example, at Dell, I wound up doing paper prediction, which is figuring out how much paper they'll be using in six months. But I used tarot cards to help me make my business predictions. After I left, I meant to go back to work, but my part-time reading business got bigger and bigger and that was twenty-one years ago.

How did you get to be so good at tarot? Years of practice, doing it eight to ten hours a day. I can teach everyone but the most obstinate or ignorant people to be good. Cards are simple. You stick with them and you stick with the questions, and what you don't know you ask people.

I have just opened the John Green Psychic Center in Hollywood, where people can learn how to do it for free. Some are charging a fortune for this, but I believe everyone should have access to this information in a way that is affordable and interesting.

How accurate are you? Being a psychic, you're always guessing, and you don't know how right you are until the end of the race. How accurate I am depends on how well I know the person and the field, how well I've been briefed on the issue, and how familiar I am with that kind of question. The cards keep me from being very wrong.

But most psychics claim they don't need any background information on the person they're reading. It's all well and good to read someone cold and throw something off the top of your head about how their relationship with their parents might be affecting their current status. But if you want to tell somebody whether their company is going to get a friendly takeover, you'd better read up on facts.

Give me someone's first name and birthday and I'll tell you what he will do in a business venture. But if you want to know what the other side is going to do in detail—his first reaction, his second reaction—then I have to know a lot more background.

What irritates you most about some clients?
They'll ask me, "Will I be rich?" That's not a good question. "What is my best course of action for making money in the next quarter or the next year?" is much better. Or they ask, "When will I be married?" when they should be asking, "How will I build a successful long-term relationship?"

JUDY HEVENLY

11955 MISSOURI AVENUE, #10
LOS ANGELES, CALIFORNIA 90025
(310) 820-7280
FAX: (310) 820-3286

Jack McCarthy/News Photos

A Hollywood psychic who is best known for the accuracy of her annual Oscar predictions.

Do Hollywood people pay psychics a lot of money? Here's something about top Hollywood people that will break your heart when I tell you the truth. None of them ever pay. You cannot make a living with Hollywood stars and wealthy people: They will not pay you. They come up in their limos. They've forgotten their purse, or they feel that you should give a reading to them for nothing. I make the majority of money from blue-collar working people. The big shots and stars don't pay.

Is it important for you to make money? I learned as a child that money isn't everything. When I was growing up in South Africa, I told my mother, "One day I'm going to be a big movie star." She said, "That can't be, because we're too poor." But I learned there was something more than money or fame, and that's your inner self. I learned to close my eyes and listen to my inner voice, the God within.

Do you have many famous clients? I have met and read for many celebrities, including Ronald and Nancy Reagan, Jaclyn Smith, Bob Hope, Sean Connery. I was invited to Buckingham Palace twice after I made accurate predictions for the royal family. But not all of my clients are in Hollywood; some are in other parts of America—small towns that nobody can reach—but I talk with the people over the phone.

What are you best known for? Every year I make Oscar predictions that are broadcast all over the world. I am often 80, 90, sometimes 100 percent accurate. Because of my knowledge of the film business—I studied movie making at UCLA—and because I help to finance movies on the side, I am able to tune in easily.

How does word come to you—and how do you get it out? Every day I get up at four-thirty to meditate and pray for my clients. But about a week before the Oscars, Oscar information is given to me. Then, each year now, the press calls me, and I tell them what I see for the awards.

Were any of your family members in the film business? My former husband, whom I met when I left South Africa and moved to London at eighteen. I bought my wedding dress two weeks before I met him! I just knew I was going to get married. He was a screenwriter for Warner Brothers working in London. He wrote the TV series *The FBI.*

With your interest in films, have you ever been in any movies? I came to the United States in 1968. I got my dream then of being in the movies—although not of being a star—when I was spotted by the man who discovered the Beatles. I ended up in a small role, and that led to another bit part in a movie with Shirley MacLaine called *The Yellow Rolls-Royce.*

Did someone help you develop your mysticism?
My father was in the funeral business for a while. He came
into contact with people who were dead. He was the one
who taught me as a child to close my eyes and go within.

***Do you think your being from South Africa had
something to do with your development in this
area?*** Yes, being from a land of magic and mysticism en-
hanced my psychic abilities. Also, it's a simpler life there.
Psychics can accept the voice of intuition. Here in America
there are too many distractions that prevent you from hearing that voice.

Did you train as a psychic? I joined an institute where
they had all the young up-and-coming psychics, people who
later became well known. We started off at five dollars a
reading. If we made three or four mistakes, we were out. If
we made bad predictions, those were considered mistakes.
We gave thirty readings a day on Saturday and Sunday. I
was guided by a very active inner voice saying to me, "Tell
them this! Tell them that!" Now, I still use my inner voice,
and I sometimes use the tarot cards. When I first began,
though, I was using automatic handwriting.

What do you tell your clients? For most of my movie
and business clients, I am like a poor man's psychiatrist,
giving them predictions. Celebrities rely on what I say, but
I only make suggestions, such as "Why don't you try meditation?" or "Why don't you try being more self-reliant and
look for the answers within yourself rather than always running off to a psychic?"

What is your blue dot meditation? I have also become well known for my blue dot meditation, which the
National Enquirer runs on a regular basis and which I also
use with clients. I energize this dot with Laura Steele* in
New York, and working from the East and West coasts, we
put our thought energy into it. When people touch the dot,
if they believe hard enough, their thoughts will make their
wishes happen.

---

*See page 148.

Has it worked? By touching this dot, six people around the world have won the lottery. One won the New York State Lottery for 2.7 million dollars. Others have gotten a new car, children have used it to pass exams, others have won a trip.

What is the best advice you give people? When my clients are trying to make a decision, I often say to them, "Imagine yes in one hand and no in the other. And then ask your higher self to raise the hand that has the correct answer."

Do you encourage people to meditate? Yes, because it helps people to develop their own psychic powers. It activates that little voice that we don't hear too much. When you meditate, you touch your higher self, and the God within will bring you what you need. Put God first in your life, and you will get everything you need.

KENNY KINGSTON

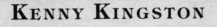

POST OFFICE BOX 1857
STUDIO CITY, CALIFORNIA 91614
(213) 650-7007
FAX: (213) 650-7008*10

Harry Langdon

*Called the psychic to the stars, he has
read for Marilyn Monroe, Lucille Ball,
the Duke and Duchess of Windsor, and
other celebrities—many of whom he
says he has spoken to after they died.*

***Is there still a strong interest in your relation-
ship with Marilyn Monroe?*** The one client everyone
usually always wants to know about is Marilyn Monroe. She
was a great believer in the psychic world, and I was her one
and only psychic. I gave her many readings when we both
lived in San Francisco in the mid-1950s. We worked in person and by telephone for about eight years until her passing.

Did she visit you or call you? Both, but frequently,
I'd pick up the phone and hear, "Hello, you, it's me." That

was the code she used, and she'd whisper it in her breathy voice.

Was she a happy person? No, Marilyn was a very troubled woman. One thing that bothered her was what she was most famous for: her sexuality. She told me, "I look at other women's figures all the time. Am I a lesbian?"

She seemed to have everything: looks, money, fame. What else did she want? Another thing that troubled her was her inability to have "little people," as she called children. She had had several miscarriages in her life.

She was also deeply affected by the death in 1960 of Clark Gable. He passed on shortly after filming of *The Misfits* was completed. She felt she had made him work too hard to make up for her acting and that she had brought about his passing.

Do you think she committed suicide? Definitely not. She told me during a recent conversation from the other side, "I was just so tired—I never meant to take so many pills with drinks. It was an accident."

What about Lucille Ball? I was her friend for forty years and later her medium. For Lucy, life hadn't been what she wanted either, and she was also disappointed.

A few weeks before she died, she participated in a séance with me. She believed in the afterlife and made contacts with her first husband, Desi, and with Joan Crawford, who was a good friend of hers.

What relationship did you have with Mae West? Some of my earliest memories are of Mae, who taught me to be clairaudient when I was about six years old. In fact, at that age, I was giving psychic advice to the world's most famous sex symbol!

How did that come about? She would call—she was friendly with my mother—and tell me to say the first thing that popped into my head, like yes or no, without thinking about it. I realize now that she was encouraging me to listen to the sound of a voice and pick up psychic vibrations from it.

She started with simple questions, but I gave her lengthy answers, which I now know were actually messages from the spirit world.

Do you have any mementos in addition to memories from all these people? I have a gold candelabra given to me by Marilyn Monroe, a silver candleholder from Tallulah Bankhead, a gold picture frame from the duchess of Windsor, a jeweled throne chair from Clifton Webb, *objets d'art* from Greta Garbo, and gifts from many other people.

Have you been in any contact with these people since they've passed on? Yes, I am able to communicate with my "Sweet Spirits," as I call those who pass on. When I'm in a semitrance, I can pick up voices from the spirit world. I believe there is no such thing as death, only a passing into a dimension—like crossing a bridge or going into another room—that I call Paradise.

What have these celebrities told you after they passed on? I have a book out called *I Still Talk To* about my association with various celebrities while they were on earthplane. In it, I describe how Humphrey Bogart reports that he's been reborn as a boy in Boston, etc.

What about Elvis? Oh yes, he's in there, too. Elvis's mother told me she was most upset about the wedding of her granddaughter to Michael Jackson. She couldn't understand why her granddaughter married such a freak. She also told me that the drugs and alcohol didn't kill her son, Elvis. She persuaded him to join her on the other side because she was lonely, and he decided to be with her.

Have you talked to others since they died? Michael Landon told me he will continue to aid and comfort other cancer patients. I've reached Jack the Ripper, but I refuse to try to contact people who died suddenly and violently like John Lennon. I try to be a gentleman. Let them rest. They've had a hard enough life on earth.

What do you think of when you look back on your accomplishments in life? So much has happened in my life, and now I can talk about it freely. In past years, psychics had to be closet psychics, but nobody thinks we're crazy today.

I'm proud of all the people I've helped personally as well as through my books and TV performances—I've hosted my own TV series twice—and my Kenny Kingston Psychic Hot Line.

I love to travel—I have a white Jaguar with the license plate SEERKK!—and I'm going to see the pope and the royal family on my next trip abroad.

What are you proudest of? When I was considering moving to San Francisco, Marion Davies, the mistress of William Randolph Hearst, told me, "You will never be accepted in San Francisco. It's a blue blood city. It's unfriendly, and nobody calls anybody by their first name." And I said, "I'm going to date the debutantes and buy a house on Pacific Heights, and I'm going to master this city. I don't care how long it takes me."

Did you? Absolutely. I had it all there and did what they said I couldn't do. But then I felt I needed new challenges and moved to Los Angeles. And when I went back to San Francisco to visit, the current mayor named August 1, 1994, Kenny Kingston Day.

ARMAND MARCOTTE

10054 BUTTE STREET
MESA, ARIZONA 85207
(602) 380-6230

*He calls himself an all-purpose psychic,
and his most famous client was John
Wayne.*

What was your relationship with John Wayne?
I read for him for about ten years, giving him personal as
well as business advice. He used to buy my ticket and fly
me to his place in Durango for readings. He wanted to put
me in one of his movies, but I turned it down because I'm
not an actor. I'm a psychic.

***You went into business with him also. How did
that happen?*** For fifteen years, I owned a cosmetology
school, Armand's Beauty College in Dana Point, California,
and Portland, Maine. I developed a cream formula, called

Hair Trigger, and he used it and it grew hair. So he invested in it and did the first commercial for it.

When was the last time you spoke to John Wayne? He called me one New Year's and said he was going into the hospital that week. He wanted to know what was going to happen to him and whether he would die from the operation.

I told him, "Duke, you're going in for a heart operation, but they'll find something wrong with you and they'll close you up and you'll be in the hospital for a while."

John Wayne had several bouts of cancer at the end. Did he ever ask you how he'd fare? Yes. He said, "Armand, I want you to tell me when I'm going to pass over." And I said, "I don't do that. But you should watch yourself around your birthday. If you survive that you'll be all right." And he died a couple of weeks after his birthday.

Have you had other celebrity clients? He was my most famous client and friend, but I've had a lot of big people and a lot of little people, too. Another star I used to do was Natalie Wood, but I worked through her maid. She would send her maid, who would come to me and ask me questions that Miss Wood wanted to know. I thought it was weird at the time, but in those days, a lot of people kept it in the closet that they wanted advice from a psychic. But John Wayne didn't.

Do you predict the future for your clients? Not really. I usually see two paths that can be taken and the consequences of both. I let clients choose their own destiny.

I have always tried to limit readings not to general predictions but to information that would help people make important life decisions, steer them away from danger, or help them to solve other personal problems.

How do you prepare for personal readings? First, I relax my mind. I am most comfortable in my own surroundings because my guides are stronger there. I prefer to know nothing about the clients. When they arrive, I ask for personal objects—preferably metal—that are intimately associated with them. I also ask for birth dates.

You've also done a lot of crime cases. What type

of information do you like to know in advance? I like to know the sex and date of disappearance of the victim before I start working with the police on the case. It seems to formulate the person in my mind. I get flashes of their form and personality. My mind begins to see shapes as others see clouds, and soon I can see clearly what has happened to this individual.

Can you be more specific? Sometimes I see myself floating above my head, completely out of my body, looking into the person's life. Sometimes I hear words or noises. In other cases, I see events, like on television.

When the spirits of murdered people come to me, I permit them partial use of my body, mainly the vocal chords, so they can tell me what happened.

Are you intuitive about those you know personally? Yes, and it started long before I became a professional psychic. Years ago, I had a horrible premonition about my cleaning lady, Valerie Montes. I saw a vision of her bloody and mutilated body in a woody area.

Did you tell her? Oh, I begged her not to leave her house. I advised her that I saw danger around her and saw her getting into a car and not returning. Then I saw the authorities arresting her husband. That Sunday, a news story of her vicious murder appeared in the local paper.

How were you able to help the investigation? Using her ring as a psychometric object, I almost immediately saw Valerie before me. She admitted that she should have listened to me, that she had been angry with her husband, that he would be called in for questioning but that he did not kill her.

She shared the details of the gruesome death at the hands of three youths on drugs with a machete. One young man knew her, and she asked me to try to find him so he could tell the police who the others were. I did, and the case was solved.

How did you become known to the public? Shortly after Valerie's murder, I was written up in the local newspaper for my psychic abilities. I had already assisted the police in other murder cases.

I also became known in my community when a professor at a local college approached me for a reading. He was a skeptic and hoped to prove me a fake. He sent about twenty of his students to see me over a period of two years and later determined that I was at least 80 percent accurate.

Of course now that I've been featured many times on *Unsolved Mysteries* and programs like *20/20, The Other Side,* and *Sightings,* people know me.

Tell us about your childhood. Did others view you as different? Yes, I was always treated that way by other children and adults. My psychic abilities frightened others, so I held them in check and learned to turn them on and off at will.

Did your abilities upset your family? I have been aware of my abilities to see into the future as well as in the past since I was four or five, so I guess my family knew it from then on too. My mother was frightened by my foreseeing events and sensing details of people's lives. She took me to a priest at an early age. The good padre tried to convince her that I was just imaginative. I, of course, knew better. After that, I tried to hide what I was thinking from my family.

Maria Papapetros

141 EAST 55TH STREET, APT. 5H
NEW YORK, NEW YORK 10022
(212) 935-4441

Michael Tighe

She was the psychic advisor to the movie The Butcher's Wife, *and she has read for many top Hollywood stars.*

With your clientele of Hollywood movie stars and film executives, why did you recently leave Los Angeles and move to New York? It was the earthquake. I say it up front. Others hide it. My clients in L.A. used to ask me about their love lives and careers. Now, when they call for a reading, they all want to see what's going to happen with earthquakes and where are they going to move to. People ask me, "Maria, when?"

Won't it interfere with your business to be in New York? They say, "Maria, why are you moving to New York when you have such a career in L.A.?" The film people are in New York also. Film is made everywhere. Now I can work easier with Europe.

***What did you do for the movie crew in* The Butcher's Wife?** The movie is about a housewife who is a psychic. I kept up the psychic vibrations on the set. I did a lot of readings. Many of the people were not believers and they were working on something they did not know anything about. I taught the cast members to understand and not to be afraid of psychics. I wanted them to know what it felt like to be psychic and to be read by a psychic.

Did you read for all the people on the set? Everybody but Jeff Daniels. His part was an unbeliever in the film so we had to keep him an unbeliever.

What was your relationship with Demi Moore? She's very professional. Such a hard-working girl. I was in the trailer with her for three months, training her how to be a psychic. I wanted her to experience what it was like to give a reading so she could read for the movie. I did meditation exercises with her to help her tune into her psychic frequencies.

Is she a believer? She was genuinely interested in all this. She's very sensitive. She could make a wonderful living as a psychic. She has a very powerful soul.

How did you get the job working on the movie? Through the producers; they came for a reading, and they started talking about a project. And then the director came by himself, and he did not know the others had come to me, and they didn't know he had.

When they asked you to work for the movie, did you jump at the chance? I said, "It is time for the psychic to be out of the closet. I will do it if it will become public. I don't want to be behind closed doors anymore." And they said, "Go ahead."

I am the first psychic to ever receive an on-screen credit. I was called a psychic consultant.

It's been written that you not only read for Demi Moore, but Kim Basinger, Mary Steenburgen, Vanessa Williams, Irene Papas, and others. Is it

true? I cannot say it, but they say it. That's why the stars see me; because I don't talk about them.

I read for everybody, not just stars. I have many regular clients from word of mouth, too.

*What did you do with the movie **Ghost?*** I worked strictly with the producer. She was a client, and she would come to me about her projects. I did not work with the actors.

What are some other high-profile things that you've done in the metaphysical area? I was consulted by the Department of Justice and the Department of State on the Josef Mengele case.

I had a lot of involvement in trying to get the people out in the Jim Jones case.

And they had no clues, absolutely no clues, on the Hillside Strangler case. And I gave them a description, and I said there were two people instead of one, which everyone was saying. And I said they were grease monkeys, which was true, and I described the identities and the addresses to the police department of things that would occur, and they did.

Do you consider yourself a mind reader? No, I do not read minds, I read frequencies. Just reading another person's mind makes for a great Las Vegas act but you cannot predict anything that way.

A good reading looks to the future and gives you warnings. It offers advice on how to manipulate the future so nothing bad should happen. I give someone the choices as I see them because I am not a fatalist. We do have choices.

Are there any clients you've turned down? A Colombian man brought me two hundred fifty thousand dollars in a bag and asked me to find his brother, whose plane was missing. I told him I couldn't take his money because the plane had disappeared into the ocean and his brother could not be found.

Then the man's mother came to me and begged me to find her son. And I said, "Listen. It cannot be done. I'm a mother who lost her child and I don't want to hurt any mother." I have to tell them this: "I cannot bring him back."

Why did they think he was still alive? The family

kept seeing fortune-tellers who would tell them, "He is alive. He has amnesia." They would pay me anything to find him alive. But I said, "He's dead, and the plane went down, and he's in the ocean." They were hoping that he had been washed up somewhere and was alive. And I was accurate, and eventually his clothes were found in that particular area, and they found the plane, too.

Do you feel for your clients' problems? When I first started my career, I could read people, but not knowing about meditation, I would carry the physical things they were feeling, like shoulder pain. I felt so sorry for them that I wanted to give them more. I would walk around with their pains and anxieties.

Then I learned how to be objective. It is extremely important in a psychic reading to separate things, and now I do not store information. I do not need to make a mental file. Now I can tune them out afterward. It is no good to remember everything.

How do you feel about being wrong sometimes? I do not play God. I am open to being wrong. I told one girl that her husband was going to give her a gold Cadillac for Christmas. She told me, "No, Maria, he gave me one last year." I said, "But this year, he will give you an antique gold Cadillac."

She came to see me after Christmas and said, "Maria, you were right. He gave me an antique gold Cadillac." I looked out the window to see it but she shook her hand. "No, see, it's a gold Cadillac charm for my *bracelet*."

How do you come upon your predictions? I just know. I use psychometry, but I don't go anywhere [astral travel]. I'm open to guides. I do not want to see pictures because then I have to put my own interpretation on them.

A psychic reading is like a radio tuning. I tune into the person's frequency and pick up the wavelength. When I pick up a piece of jewelry, I read the waves.

When did you learn you were psychic? I came to America at eighteen. Then I owned a beauty salon in Los Angeles. After I visited a psychic, she told me I was psychic. I said, "Isn't everybody?"

One day she suggested we exchange a session. She told

me to pick up an object and tell her what I felt. I did—and surprised myself. I began to give readings for my friends, and it got so out of hand that I closed the salon. I've been busy ever since.

Do you think everyone is psychic? If you have a soul, you're psychic. Everybody uses their abilities. We go to the closet in the morning. Which dress to wear? We're talking to the psychic part of us. If everyone recognized their own talents, I'd have a lot more professional competition.

Do you do anything besides readings? I teach seminars all over America. I fly back and forth between my offices in New York, Los Angeles, San Francisco, San Antonio, Houston, and the Hamptons. I teach guided visualization meditation to help people get in touch with their psychic space. I teach people how to do a psychic reading for themselves and others in one day. And when people ask me, "Maria, why should I develop my psychic ability?" I say, "You use it for everyday living so you get more mileage out of life."

LOU WRIGHT

2216 BAYARD PARK DRIVE
EVANSVILLE, INDIANA 47714
(812) 471-9515

*Her most famous client was
Elvis Presley.*

What was your relationship with Elvis? I knew him from 1973 until his death. I met him through a nurse whose son was in his entourage. I started working with him on his Aloha Hawaii comeback tour. Then, for four years, I was his friend and personal psychic.

How often were you in contact with him? He would pay for me to fly or drive down to Memphis and he would fly me to various appearances of his. I spoke with him sometimes two and three times a day. When I moved from Indiana to Denver in 1976, he would fly out there for his peanut butter sandwiches—and to see me.

Did people know you were Elvis's psychic? I never told anyone I was his main psychic until after his death.

Even then, I didn't reveal it. It came out from those people who were writing books and investigating every aspect of his life.

Have you heard from him since he died? I have continued to receive messages from him. On occasion, I'll get in the car and he'll come on the radio, and it's like he's saying, "It's going to be OK." Sometimes I hear his voice, but I don't sit down and have long conversations with Elvis.

What kind of things did you discuss during your readings with him? He wanted to know about record labels, contracts, numbers, dates to come out with something, dates to talk to someone, and colors.

Colors? Yes. If Elvis was going to be appearing someplace, he wanted to know what color jumpsuits to wear. Or what colors were best to use for his record labels.

What kind of problems did he have? They weren't that different from anyone else's. Basically he was lonely, looking for that one right relationship. He was always very concerned about his fans. It was unreal the way he wanted to be sure he pleased his fans. The man was absolutely wonderful.

Was he involved in the metaphysical? Very much so. We talked a lot about that, religion, and health matters. When he died, he was reading an Edgar Cayce book called *Psychic Energy*.

How do you work? I can turn my psychic abilities on and off. It's like sipping a drink of water. I can drink and then put the glass down. To get started, all I need is a voice, a name, or an object, and it turns on my abilities.

Do clients ask you a lot of questions? When people come in, I answer the majority of their questions without their asking. At the end, I allow them to ask me unlimited questions, but it usually isn't necessary because I've already answered them.

How often do you see your clients? I can see ahead six months to a year, so my clients usually don't contact me more than once a year.

My weekly schedule is, I work four days a week, starting on those days at six A.M. working until midnight.

Do skeptics make you uncomfortable? I don't mind skeptics. I try to help everyone. Psychics have to work harder than most people to prove themselves. I have worked very hard to prove my legitimacy. If I were a phony, I'd be scared spitless. But I'm confident about my abilities. If I looked at questions people ask me as if they were secretly trying to trip me up, it would make me nervous.

Who are your clients? They include everyone right up to CEOs of large companies. I also worked with people like the representative of the manufacturer of the stealth bomber, telling them what the bidding would be with the government, what the government officials would go for, and what the government personalities were like so they could bid properly. And I was right on.

Have you worked on any missing persons cases? Many. I found a little girl in Denver—I found her alive—and I correctly described the abductor. I said the child would be found in a bathroom, and she was found in an outhouse.

I found a missing divorcée, and while other psychics said she was being held hostage, I said, "No. Her body is at the bottom of Cherrycreek Dam, with a rock on her foot." And that's where and how they found her.

How accurate are you? I'm 80 to 90 percent accurate. I wouldn't want to be 100 percent accurate—it's too scary, especially to know when someone will die. I knew Elvis was going to die.

Does someone help give you your predictions? They come from the guardian angels, who I feel are of God. When I hear their voices, I put it in human words. I'm sure that I occasionally make mistakes in the translation. I have my misses, sometimes on the stupidest little things, but that's the way it goes.

When did you first see these spirits or guardian angels? As a child, I had invisible friends, very real little spirit playmates who were invisible to my family. They had no sex and no names. I knew the difference from their voices.

I was brought up in a rural area, and I had no playmates, so my guardian angels were my friends. My sister would say, "Please don't walk down the street and talk to yourself. People think you're kookie anyway." But I wasn't talking to *myself*. I was talking to my guardian angels.

Have they stayed with you? Oh yes, I still have them. The voices I hear now were the voices I heard then. They've grown into lifelong guardian angels for me.

Have you ever seen them? Only on one occasion, and to be honest, it really frightened me. I was going through a rather turbulent time in my life, and I woke up from a dead sleep and found this person sitting on my bed in a white robe and a white turban, who said, "Don't be afraid; this will pass, and you're learning some very wonderful lessons."

Do you like being psychic? At times it's a cross to bear, especially when I get a sinking and helpless feeling if I wake up in the middle of the night with images of a plane crash I know I can't stop. Or when I tell the police where they will find the body of a missing child. Still I believe my consultations have prevented suicides, saved marriages, and improved health.

Do you tell people everything you see? I tell them what I see in their futures, but I also tell them that if it isn't something they want, they have the potential to change it, and they can pray about it. Only birth, death, and meeting certain people are predetermined. Careers, finances, can all be changed. People are in charge of their own lives.

What do you tell people if you see a grim future? I don't have time to paint a fairy tale for people because I'm too busy. I had a lady in here the other day, and she said, "When I came to you, you told me that there was going to be some big hurt in my life the next month. And my daughter was killed then."

How religious are you? I'm like a computer—and God turns me on. I believe that God is my agent. As long as I give glory to God, my gift will be with me.

I give a prayer card out to my clients. Many ministers, priests, and nuns come to me, and they have career questions for me as well as personal ones.

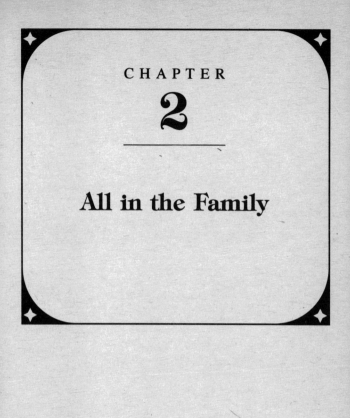

CHAPTER

2

All in the Family

MARIAN BELUSHI-MILES

POST OFFOCE BOX 1395
ADDISON, ILLINOIS 60101
(708) 628-1187

Adam Eichhorst

Sometimes called the "samurai psychic," she's the sister of actor Jim Belushi and the late actor John Belushi.

Do you feel that your family is a factor in your success? Being a Belushi may help get people interested in me at first, but if I wasn't good, they wouldn't come back. I think it also helps me professionally that I'm a dramatic person, and that runs in the family, because two of my brothers are or were famous actors.

Besides your two famous brothers, are others in your family in the movie business? My third brother, who has been an air-conditioning repairman, is now becoming a photographer on movie sets. And my son by my first marriage is a lighting and electrical grip on movies.

Did you ever have any premonitions of disaster for your immediate family? Five years ago, I saw my mother's death before it happened. And I saw John's death eight days before it occurred.

Are you willing to talk about John? All right. He was two years younger than me, and we were very close. I believe the reason we were bonded like twins was that we were also together in a past life.

One day in 1982, I was talking to him on the phone for about two hours, and I picked up that he was going to die. I told him, "I'm never going to see you again in this life," and I was crying and couldn't hang up the phone. He told me he loved me and that I was "his bestest sister," which he always said to me, starting when I was about seven and he was five. And I would always say, "But I'm your only sister, so that's not fair." Only this last time when he said it, I was too upset to say a thing.

How did your psychic ability develop? When I was about four, I tuned in psychically about my family. I saw that my oldest brother Jim was going to be rich and famous, but when I told him, he thought I had him mixed up with John!

Did your family think you were psychic? I don't think they really believed it until I was sixteen. Then the phone rang one day and I started screaming, "Don't answer it! It's Uncle Chris saying Grandma died!" And it was.

By then, my telepathy included strangers as well as friends, and I was so accurate, everyone was coming up to me for advice. I became like Dear Abby!

Describe how you work. When I'm tuned in, I can see flashes or pictures, and I see and I feel things, like speeded-up frames in a movie. At sessions, I use psychometry, too. I ask people to bring pictures of someone in their lives they'd like to know more about, and I hold the pictures and tell them what I see. I also pick up on jewelry, but I'm best with pictures.

Do you use cards? Yes, but regular ones, not tarot. I think tarot represents the dark satanic side of being a psychic. Regular cards don't have anything except the vibrations that I put on them. Most psychics pick up on cards or on the person, but I pick up on both the person and the cards at the same time.

Have you done any crime cases? I helped a father find his son who was missing for five years. He had been involved in a custody dispute, and his wife stole the child. He had no idea where she took him. The police had nothing to go on because we learned later that the mother had taken a job working with a church for cash so there was no paper trail.

What did you have to go on? The only photograph the father had was of his boy when he was two. I held this photo and zoomed in that the boy was in Florida, near a tower and a lake, and that "lake" also factored into the picture. The police started looking in Lakeland, Florida, and found him exactly where I said he would be.

What made you become a professional psychic? I was originally a hair stylist, and people were asking me questions even before they knew I was psychic. They were just drawn to me.

While I was working, I took classes to develop my God-given ability, but I had a son to support, so I couldn't just quit everything and go into business.

When did you become professional? After five years of studying, I went professional and quit the hair business totally. This is what I always wanted to do. Being a psychic wasn't an afterthought. My husband, Rodney, is my manager, and he helps me with the business end.

What is your specialty? I'm excellent in legal matters. People give me court papers or papers if they're buying a house, going bankrupt, or getting divorced, and I can see what they should do, what they should change, what they should tell their lawyers, or if the vibes are bad.

I'm also superb with financial deals and have a lot of corporate clients who I help on business choices. For example, I'll tell them if I don't feel good about the person they're dealing with and if they should go to somebody else.

I also have a lot of doctors and psychologists who come to me. I have a plastic surgeon, a sex therapist, and a psychoanalyst who specializes in counseling Vietnam veterans for flashbacks.

Is there any question you don't like to hear from people? Many people ask me whether they will win the lottery. Don't they want to know more about their future than that? Anyway, gambling is on Satan's side, and I don't want to be a party to that. I use my gift for positive things, to teach and help people and guide them.

What do you like best about your work? I like seeing people grow mentally and spiritually. I call myself a spiritual psychic because my talent is a gift from God. I feel that is why I am here, to do this job. It is my destiny.

Give an example of someone you've helped. One of my clients was very paranoid and afraid to leave her apartment by herself, even to drive a car or go to work. It was hard to get her to come to me. But I saw her really able to do all these things, and I told her about my flashes, and she believed in me and began to believe in herself. And now she's a very functional person. It's like night and day—and that's a big thing to me.

I can teach people to be positive, to let go of negativity and make better choices and better decisions.

BERTIE MARIE CATCHINGS

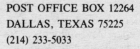

POST OFFICE BOX 12264
DALLAS, TEXAS 75225
(214) 233-5033

John Catchings

Mother of a world-famous crime psychic (the late John Catchings), this psychic detective has been called the best psychic in Texas.

What was your first psychic experience? When I was two, my mother was murdered. I was sleeping and woke in the room with her body. I didn't understand what had happened, so I approached and asked her something. Although she was dead, I remember that she responded by saying to me, "Bertie Marie, tell them I'm alive." My mother's spirit stayed around me for several years.

What did you do before you became a professional psychic? I worked as a secretary for a government office. By 1961, I had a number of psychic feelings, and sometimes I would know things about people when I was growing up. But I never considered myself a psychic.

When did you give your first reading? One morning, a co-worker invited me out to have coffee with her. She told me, "Bertie, I'm going to a fortune-teller tonight, and if my future isn't better than my past, I'm going to kill myself." I was afraid that a reader might tell her negative things that could put her over the edge. And suddenly there was like a voice speaking into my head, saying, "Why don't you read for her?"

What did you tell her? Ah, I told her some lovely things that I believed would be in her future, such as she would meet a widowed person in a short while and be married, and she would be quite wealthy, and they would live in a green two-story house by a lake where boats would go whizzing by.

Did she? Everything came true. Within six months she was married to the man that I described, and I went to visit her and the boats did go whizzing by.

How did your fame develop? After saving that woman's life, during coffee breaks all of my co-workers wanted me to give them readings, and I got used to cold coffee. Then everyone in the capitol wanted predictions, and then the governor's mansion called for me to read for the governor's wife. Eventually I was listed in *The Book of Texas Best,* where I'm credited as being the "best Texas psychic." Then Irving Wallace wrote a book called *The Book of Predictions,* and they listed me as one of the seven psychics in the book whose predictions came true.

What was that for? My accurate prediction about one of the Arab-Israeli wars.

Did any of your predictions end up in newspapers? In March 1966, three ladies called for a reading. After I told one some personal things, while she took notes, I told her I saw a man standing in a tower and shooting people and bodies falling on the ground. Then on August 1, 1966, Charles J. Whitman stood on the tower at the University of Texas and shot thirty-three passersby, killing twelve people and an unborn child. My prediction ended up in the news.

Did any others make the news? I have also been in the newspapers for accurately predicting a plane crash, finding someone missing from a nursing home, and for locating a missing two-and-a-half-year-old boy in time for him to be found alive. And I've predicted a few murders in advance, which gets the newspeople excited.

Did the fame of your son help you become known? Definitely. My son John, who became psychic after being struck by lightning, was a world-famous crime psychic. He died in 1992. He worked on hundreds of cases and appeared on *Unsolved Mysteries*, *Today*, *The Montel Williams Show*, *That's Incredible*, *PM Magazine*, *Geraldo*, and Time-Life's *Mysteries of the Unknown*—they even did a section on him.

Are you still in contact with him? Very much so, through mental telepathy and in dreams, even though he's on the other side.

When was the first time you heard him talk to you? We used to have a joke that we should never fly in the same airplane because the world would lose the two greatest psychics. The first time I was aware that he was talking to me, I was on an airplane. And I could hear his voice in my head saying, "Mama, now we can fly together."

Did he say anything else then? He said, "Mama, I'm one of your guardian angels now. They told me that you deserve to have me as your angel because you were always there for me when I needed you."

Do you ask your clients for any special information? I ask them for their four favorite colors. For example, people who like red usually have a lot of energy, organize things well, know how to come in out of the rain, and quit a job or relationship that's not right.

What do you do for your clients? I read their palms, study their auras, use astrology, use photographs they bring me for auras and psychometry, and do handwriting analysis. Before a session I have people fill out a card for me. Then I hold it and I can pick up things about them from that.

JILL DAHNE

16425 COLLINS AVENUE
MIAMI BEACH, FLORIDA 33160
(305) 949-4444
FAX: (305) 940-1515

The daughter of a famous psychic, Micki Dahne, this love psychic has predicted over two hundred marriages and is in Ripley's Believe It or Not.

Why are you called a love psychic? Not only clients but all my girlfriends consult me. All someone has to do is just say someone's name, and I can visualize everything about that person. I give my friends the date and time when the man they like will call, when they will make up after a fight, that sort of thing.

Have you predicted any weddings? Over two hundred of them—and I've been invited to every single one of them! When good predictions come true, many happy people want to give me presents. Some want to send money, but I tell them to give it to charity instead.

What do people ask a love psychic? "Will he marry this other woman?" Or "Where is my relationship going?" Or men call and ask, "Is she cheating?"

What do you tell them? Only what is true, and that's not always what they want to hear. Most of the time I make people happy, but sometimes the truth does hurt. Some people just don't want to see reality. They know something is going on, but they don't want to look at the truth.

Don't you want to make people happy? I'm not going to tell someone something untrue just to make them happy for the day. I'm known for my accuracy, and I don't want to break that. So I won't lie and tell people what they want to hear—that a boyfriend is coming back, that he will marry them. I tell them what's going to happen.

Are they upset? Yeah. Sometimes they hang up on me. But then they call back in a few months and say, "You were right. He didn't leave his wife for me."

Give an example of someone you didn't make happy. One time a woman called me, and I didn't know her husband was listening on the phone. I told her that her husband was cheating on her, and there was a child out there by this other woman. I gave her the name of the other woman. She went to her rival's house and found out she had a baby by her husband. She was unhappy about it, and the husband also called and screamed at me because he knew that I was the one who told her.

When was it first obvious that you had psychic abilities? I was kicked out of kindergarten for telling a teacher what she was about to write on the board before she wrote it. I was suspended for ten days. The teacher thought I was a witch.

Didn't everyone expect you to be psychic because your mother has been a famous psychic for so many years? Yeah, I guess I got it from her. When I was young, she never had to call my name. Before the words came out, I would turn around or just come to her.

What famous prediction did you make while you were still a teenager? In 1977, when I was thirteen, I was doing a radio show with my mom. During one broadcast, I predicted the exact date of the Muslim attack on Washington, March 9, 1977, when the Hanafi Muslims took over three Washington buildings. Afterward, I was written up everywhere as "amazing teenage psychic" and also in *Ripley's Believe It or Not: Ghosts and Goblins.*

What do you like best and least about being psychic? I love to help people, but I also don't like to see tragedies. But they can come along with the happy endings.

Can you give an example? Once a gentleman came all the way to Florida from Texas just to see me. I saw that he was dying. It had something to do with his heart. I started crying. As soon as he returned to his home state, he had a heart attack and died. That incident hurt me, and sometimes it hurts to feel so much.

What do you like about being psychic? It's fun to play psychic practical jokes. I'm telekinetic, which means I move things. One time I made a fan start moving in a restaurant. Another time I made someone's earring fall off.

What don't you like about it? Doing radio and working too intensely with hundreds of thousands of people listening. Last year I had my own two-hour radio show until the station was sold. It was often a strain to sit on the phone all day while the whole world is listening. Plus, with all those people listening, it is important to be right.

Are you good at bringing people together like your mother does? Yes, I've brought families together too. One time I told someone from Los Angeles about her sister. She claimed she didn't have a sister. Then she asked her mom, who told her that she had a sister in Ohio.

Have you done any missing persons cases? A woman from Arkansas phoned me about her missing husband. He wanted to leave her—he had been cheating on her—and he disappeared one day. The police hadn't been able to locate him, and she put a reward out for him.

I gave the right number of the address where he was and said I saw a yellow lane. He was found on Goldilocks Lane, and of course, goldilocks are yellow. He was living with the other woman when they found him, but he ended up coming back to his wife.

Did you collect the reward? No, because I don't like taking money in those cases. I told them to give it to charity. My reward was, they got back together and now they're happy.

MICKI DAHNE

16425 COLLINS AVENUE
MIAMI BEACH, FLORIDA 33160
(305) 949-4444
FAX: (305) 940-1515

She specializes in helping missing children and their parents find each other, and she gained worldwide fame when she predicted two plane crashes as well as Watergate.

How did your psychic abilities develop? My father was vice president of theaters owned by Warner Brothers in New York, and I was always around show business people. Many of them believed in psychics, although they never said anything.

My mother went to a psychic, but she didn't want me to *be* one. When I said something was going to happen, my mother would say, "You're starting rumors."

Did you act differently as a child? I'm very dyslexic, and I was left back in kindergarten and fourth grade, but in my day who knew from dyslexic?

Being left back and constantly scolded by my mother, I used to talk to people who weren't there, and my mother would get very aggravated and angry. I used to think my name was a Yiddish expression meaning "Don't hit her in the head," because my grandmother said that so often to my mother in Yiddish.

What is an early psychic recollection of yours? I remember one day shouting at my mother, "Your pearls!" And I heard a firecracker and kept holding my ears. It turned out to be the day Pearl Harbor was bombed. So I got hit in the head again.

When did you realize that your predictions weren't accidents? I didn't really consider myself to be psychic until my first husband—I've had seven since—died in 1971 of Hodgkins. While he was sick, things kept happening the way I thought they were going to happen. But if I told him what I knew, he would say, "Oy, another nut."

Give some examples of your specialty. Finding lost children and finding adopted children's biological parents. One woman came to me, and I suddenly saw a redheaded baby. I said, "Why did you give away the redheaded baby?" And she broke out crying.

Did you find the redheaded baby? With the information I gave her, she eventually was able to find her daughter, a redheaded child. The baby's adoptive parents had just died, so until this woman came along, the child was all alone in the world. I really felt good; I always do when I take a family and put them back together again.

Have you put runaway teens together with their families? A mother called me because her daughter of twelve or thirteen had disappeared and she couldn't find her. I told her which street her daughter was on. I said, "She's in a motel and she's safe." Her mother found her where I said; these two guys had picked her up, and she hadn't been hurt yet, thank God.

Do you ever find people when someone else didn't know they existed? It's not that infrequent. People who come to me for other reasons don't always know that someone close is missing. For example, a woman named Suzy came to me for a reading and I asked, "Who's the adopted child who is looking for you?" And she was stunned. She didn't know what I was talking about. And I said, "There's an adopted child looking for you, and she's in Columbia, South Carolina."

So what happened? That night her mother called her and said, "Sit down. I have something to tell you. Twenty years ago I gave birth to another child, and I had to give her up. Her name is Linda, she looks just like you and she's from Columbia, South Carolina."

Did they get together? We flew Linda in to the radio station I was on. Suzy thought she was going to be on a news show, but there was Linda waiting to meet her sister Suzy for the first time. "She looks exactly like my mother," Suzy kept saying. Everyone was crying, including me.

Can you just look at someone and know something about them? One time a girl walked up to me after I spoke, and she said "Micki, how is my mother?" And I looked at her and said, "You're adopted, and your mother is a dancer, and you'd better get to her because she is about to leave for California."

And? Her mother turned out to be one of the Rockettes, and the day her daughter found her she was leaving for California. Now they're plugged in together, and they're inseparable. I'm a Micki-in-the-nick-of-time person. I've got lots of brownie points in heaven, but I can't eat them.

All your clients seem to be looking for women. Have people come to you searching for male family members? Lots of times. One man said he had been looking for his father for thirty years. I said, "He's in Corpus Christi in a nursing home." In ten minutes they found him by calling all the nursing homes in Corpus Christi. He took him home to live with him and his family.

How about someone looking for a son? A woman called me as a joke. She said, "I don't believe in psychics, but I thought I'd give you a call because my friends told me to call you."

I said, "Fine. Why do I smell Hershey bars?" And she said, "I'm leaving for Hershey, Pennsylvania, tomorrow and I can't find my boys. They've been missing for three years."

And I said, "What does Ohio have to do with it?" And she said, "My in-laws live there." And I said, "Your boys live in Texas, and I see a *C*. Does one have something wrong with his ear and the other have a hip problem?" Well, one did have something wrong with his ear, and the other had a plate in his hip.

Did she find them? She started looking for them, and one day my husband came home, got on his knees, and kissed my hand because he had just heard from the woman. "Sweetheart, she found them," he said.

It turned out the father was living in Corpus Christi, Texas, with a woman named Charlene. I scare myself sometimes! They've all just had their first Christmas together. She called me and said, "I believe in psychics now."

Have you done other kinds of psychic work? Oh, a lot. A newspaper sent me to Kansas to find things in the Jesse James house. I walked in and said, "Something is wrong with his knee." And then they found an old coin box that Mr. James had saved, and there was an old receipt from Dr. Hill for seven dollars for treating his knee.

What else happened at Jesse James's house? While I was there, I also felt a fireball coming through the window. And then we found out that a fireball had come through the window and killed James's little brother.

What have been your best-known predictions? Years ago I predicted that two American planes would crash within days of each other in the second week of September. One would be an Eastern Airlines jet that would go down in the southeastern United States.

Did they? First a TWA jetliner crashed off Greece on September 8, 1974. And three days later, an Eastern jet went down in North Carolina.

What about political predictions? When the Republican convention was down here in Florida in 1971, they asked me on radio who was going to win. And I said Nixon and Agnew. I said that Agnew would leave with his head hanging and that Nixon would have trouble with water, but I didn't think it had anything to do with Biscayne Bay, where he lived. And then came Watergate.

Terry and Linda Jamison

3614 WADE STREET
LOS ANGELES, CALIFORNIA 90066
(310) 390-5696

Photograph by Jona Frank

These twins work together with clients,
specializing in clairvoyance and
channeling through automatic writing.

How do you two work together? (Terry) When we
do phone readings, it's a three-way call. In person, we sit
side by side opposite the client.

**Because there are two of you, do you charge
more?** No, we don't double our rates. Actually, we charge
less than most psychics, so we feel people are getting two
excellent psychics for the price of one!

　(Linda) We're two channels, no waiting.

Do you receive information at the same time?
(Terry) Yes. We're working now on a murder case with a
woman whose sister was killed in London. And we both got

the same name of the killer psychically even though neither of us had ever heard his name before.

Are you two alike? I'm more the introvert, more introspective, a little more cautious, the quieter one. Linda is very outgoing, more of a risk taker, perhaps more flamboyant. But psychically, we're very similar, even how we work.

Have you had parallel experiences? (Linda) We have, starting in our late teens. We're synchronistic in our thinking. But our handwritings are very different. Terry being more introverted, her handwriting is smaller and tighter. Mine is larger, more fluid and elaborate.

Are you both married? (Terry) I was the only one who was married. Most men are threatened by our bond, but my husband wasn't.

What did you do before you began channeling people? (Linda) We were performance artists, and we owned our own theatrical company. We were comic actresses, but we started out doing robotic mime. You can imagine what people thought seeing twin robotized mannequins in the windows of places like Bonwit Teller, Bloomingdale's, and other stores.

Was your family theatrical or artistic? (Terry) Our parents—our father especially—are famous watercolorists. We were gifted, and people called us child prodigies. We could do full portraits at the age of five.

Did some crisis lead to your current calling? (Linda) We both suffered from the same chronic illness for several years.

(Terry) No one really knows whether it was mercury poisoning, lupus, arthritis, autoimmune breakdown, or what. By the time we reached our twenties, we were so ill. Medicine had failed us. We went on a long search for the cure.

We ended up studying with psychic healers who helped us in our psychic abilities and taught us to communicate with the other side. It was just the beginning of a path that opened up our psychic abilities for us. We know now that we're here on this planet with a mission of healing.

How do you do your automatic writing? (Linda)

We do not need to use automatic writing, but we like to use it as a tool because it facilitates the information we're getting.

Before either of us begins, we ask for a prayer of protection from our highest guides, goddesses, and angelic entities so we will receive only high-vibration entities through our pen.

What does it look like? My automatic writing is very beautiful, even, flowing, swirly, and embellished. It just comes out of me so smoothly. My hand just moves, and it flows out of my pen on the paper. I can write pages and pages and pages of information on any subject. The language is different from our regular language, more formal and archaic.

How does automatic writing give answers? When we are asked a "yes" or "no" question, if the answer from our guides is a "no," our hands pull backward very noticeably, sort of like a magnetic pull. If it's a "yes" answer, we continue to write. A lot of details come through on the "yes" answers.

I also find myself drawing pictures while channeling. The pictures are very geometric. I'm finding I'm doing the most amazing drawings while I'm channeling.

Was there any background or training that helped you in this channeling? (Terry) We've been practicing Buddhists for ten years, chanting for several hours a day for ten years. That's opened us up so much psychically.

(Linda) I've been told I have a numerological makeup that helps make me be good at it.

How do you help people who contact you? The way we work is more as spiritual counselors than as predictors or analysts of past lives.

(Terry) A lot of people come to us because of romantic problems. It is common for women to ask, "Is he going to come back?" "Am I going to get divorced?" "Am I going to marry again?" "When will I meet Mr. Right?" Women have been encouraged to put their happiness outside themselves.

And what do you do for them? Typically, we work with clients in terms of reclaiming their own power and helping them realize that their happiness lies within themselves.

We help them take more responsibility for developing their lives and their talents, their interests, and their intellect.

(Linda) We teach people to understand the importance of taking responsibility for having created everything in their experience. The aspects of changing one's destiny rather than being a victim. The importance of forgiveness.

Besides being twins, how do you differ from regular therapists or counselors? Immediately, without asking a client who comes in any questions, we start to channel the exact problem that person is having the moment they walk in the door. We already know why they're there. That's our gift.

What is this based on? Their childhood relationship with their parents and their past lives. And almost every time, people say, "You are uncanny. That's absolutely right!"

Can you give a specific example? (Terry) We might be able to say, "You were abused as a child," or "Your father was withholding love," or "Your parents were absentee," and we'll be absolutely right! We're not guessing. We're reading vibrations from their spirit guides.

How do people react to you? They seem to respond to our energy in an amazing way. We're used to speaking in front of large groups like television audiences. We lectured on Buddhism for a long time. Because of our theatrical background, we're used to performing. This training and experience help give us the confidence, which causes great responses.

(Linda) Our main thrust in the work we do is encouragement toward one's self-empowerment and getting in touch with one's spiritual side.

Do you predict things for your clients? (Terry) Yes, and though it gets people interested, it isn't the real heart of the matter. It's a way of intriguing people. It's interesting, but it won't change your karma to know the future or to analyze your past lives.

Hy Kaplan and Phyllis Schwartz

C/O ADVISOR ASSOCIATES
102 SANDRINGHAM ROAD
CHERRY HILL, NEW JERSEY 08003
(609) 751-1997
FAX: (609) 424-2914

This aunt-and-nephew team has a unique psychic business service, evaluating potential employees while knowing only five things about them.

How does your work differ from that of most psychics? Most answer questions from their clients like: How is my career coming? What do I do about my health? My finances? My love life?

We're looking at things from a different view. We're saying to an employer, "A hiring mistake could cost you a good deal of money. You need to know how a potential employee is going to work and how he or she is going to work with the people in this company. Are they lying on their résumés? Will they be disruptive?" And more.

How can you tell about these things? We need only five pieces of information from the company about anyone they're considering hiring: their name, age, gender, where they live—not the exact address but, say, Philadelphia, so we have less chance of tuning into other people in this country with the same name—and the position they're applying for at the company. Then we tell the client whether the person will be good for the job.

What type of problems do you tell the client about? If the person is in bad health, if they've had trouble with violence in the past, if they have any kind of personality disorder that would make it difficult for them to work in the company, if traveling will be a problem.

For example, we did a psychic reading of someone who lived an hour and a half away from the company. We cautioned the boss that the long commute could become a problem, even though the man they were considering hiring told them it wouldn't cause any difficulties. They hired him anyway, and he quit after a year because he was getting too much pressure from his wife about commuting.

What if you come up with something very personal about the person you're evaluating? We usually won't pass it on to the employer. Our rule of thumb is, we don't squeal unless it affects the job. If someone is undergoing a divorce, we don't think an employer should know about that unless it's going to cause a problem. If he's a cocaine abuser, we'll tell them, but if he's a recreational drug user, we don't.

How do you two work? My aunt and I don't talk to anybody but each other about a client. We never meet the people we evaluate, and we don't ask for a résumé. We just talk into a tape recorder. Someone, somewhere, turns on a spigot and gives us information in our heads, and then the spigot is turned off.

The hardest part is taking it off the tape and transcribing it so the typist can type it up. We have to go back and listen to the whole thing more than once.

Are two psychics better than one here? We're good on our own, but we find that doing the readings together increases our accuracies. We're almost identical psychically. We haven't disagreed on anything in twenty years. We may build on what the other says, but one of us never says red and the other says blue.

How did you two get together? Phyllis, my aunt by marriage, knew she was psychic when she was six. But I wasn't that bright. I didn't find out until I was thirty.

I am a physicist by education, and I didn't realize I was psychic—although I was. I always thought I knew certain things because I was smart.

It took a while before we both confessed our skills to each other because it wasn't the kind of thing you talked about back then. But twenty years ago, we got together at a family gathering. We discovered we had this mutual interest, and we started working together immediately.

Did you do anything other than readings? Two years later, we started a psychic radio show together. We saw that 70 percent of the questions were business ones. Eight years ago we started this service.

How did you get your first client? Our first company told us that if we could read five potential salespeople successfully, they would bring us a lot of business. We didn't know it, but they secretly gave us the names of some long-time employees who they knew well, and they threw in an accountant who didn't belong in the group at all.

We said the accountant didn't fit into the group and correctly read which of the others were problems. We saw that one man might be involved in a chemical substance situation, and it turned out he was a drug abuser who was messing up on the job. After we submitted this report, the company put us on retainer.

What are your rates? We charge fifteen hundred dollars and up for a reading on one person. We charge three thousand dollars and up for a potential CEO because these reports are up to fifteen pages so we do a lot more work. We have to analyze whether a CEO is going to interface with others, do they have the right kind of personality for board meetings, and more. We spend a couple of weeks doing these reports.

Do you offer any cheaper services? We also have something for people in a hurry who just want a quick yes–no answer. We tell them to fax us the information about a client they're trying to hire, and we'll fax them back a "yes" or "no." Even the secretary doesn't know what we're talking about. We'll play it as close as they want.

Who uses this service? One of our clients is a head-hunter. He may have a list of seventy to eighty people he thinks will be adequate for a job. He gives us the name, age, gender, where they live, and the position they apply for. And we just look at it and say, "Present him" or "Don't present him." We charge fifty dollars for every name he gives us.

Do you offer any other kinds of psychic evaluations for businesses? For some clients, we look into a whole range of corporate issues: mergers, acquisitions, business decisions, strategies, customer interfaces, team evaluation, almost anything dealing with the dynamics of businesses.

We also offer a business projection plan where we predict the future of the company ten years from now, looking at how their management team fits in, if some area is deteriorating, do they have to do something special to make something happen, that sort of thing.

How do clients learn about your services? We have brochures and mailings, but most clients come from word of mouth. It's done quietly because most people don't get up at a business convention and say, "I'm using psychics to make hiring decisions."

Could someone sue you if they found out that you said they were wrong for a job? No. Once you apply for a job, there's nothing wrong with their submitting your application to a graphologist, a private detective agency, or a psychic.

We're very legal in what we do. We guarantee that we don't see the person or their résumé. We just tell the employer what they would like to know about them.

Aren't your clients worried that some stockholders or customers will be upset that they're spending their money on psychics? We operate under conditions of strict confidentiality. Nothing on our letterhead indicates that we're psychics. The invoice we send out just reads, "one evaluation" or "consulting services."

The president of one company has us on retainer, and we don't even itemize his bill so his secretary or accountant won't know what the money is spent on.

Who in the company knows about you? Sometimes no one in the company but the boss knows. We always go to the boss first when we're soliciting an account because anyone under him or her would need to get approval and that can cause problems.

What do you say to people who think this is a strange way to hire employees? Considering how decisions are made in most offices—including the Oval Office—a psychic really isn't so weird, is it?

How do you feel about people who don't get a job because you said they weren't right for the company? These people may not be right for this position, but there may be another position they may be right for. We feel they're being *redirected,* and they'll pick up another job elsewhere.

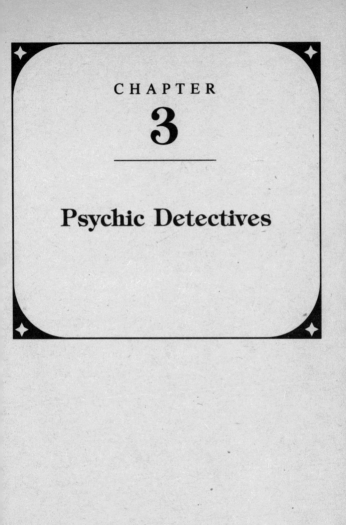

CHAPTER

3

Psychic Detectives

GRETA ALEXANDER

POST OFFICE BOX 664
DELAVAN, ILLINOIS 61734
(309) 244-8515
FAX: (309) 244-8522

Being hit by lightning was the first event that turned this housewife into a psychic who has worked on more than five hundred crime cases.

How accurate are you? I don't think people should expect psychics to be 100 percent accurate. I can't find everybody, but I can usually give people some direction as to where to look. We're not miracle workers—we're people. And skeptics—yahoos and pip-squeaks—don't bother me. I'm not worthy to judge my neighbors, and I hope my neighbors won't judge me.

How much do you charge for your police work? Nothing. I don't charge a dime. Zilch. And I don't even want publicity for it. Until a few years ago, I would only help the police if they kept my name secret, because I wasn't here for publicity. I was there to help. And if it was my kid who disappeared or had been murdered, I sure would want someone to help me.

Do you enjoy crime work? I do this work because I like helping people, although I don't find it fun. Because I get into the crime, I feel that I've been shot and stabbed and drowned thousands of times. When I'm working on a case, I feel what the victim felt, and it takes me several days to recover. I've died thousands of times.

How do you recover? I usually require two days of meditation after a big case to regain my strength. Then I let it go. After you work a case, you've got to bless it and let it up to God or else you go over it again and again.

What is your work background? I was born near Peoria, Illinois, in 1932. My dad was a farmer, so I spent a lot of time alone in the field. My hair was cut like a boy's, but every time I looked I was still a girl.

How did your family make a living? My family barely did, plucking feathers from chickens. After I married, I worked along with them for a year, getting twenty-five cents for each bird I cleaned. I'm used to working.

When did you start working? When I was eleven, I began working at a restaurant as a dishwasher. By thirteen or fourteen, I was promoted to the position of fry cook, earning twenty-five cents per hour. And I was thrilled.

How did your metaphysical life develop? I had always believed that I would die at age thirty-two, because Christ died at thirty-three. At thirty-two, however, everything changed in my life.

How? While pregnant with my fifth child, I was struck by lightning. It came through the window, wrapping the venetian blinds that had been ripped from the window around me and setting the bed on fire. I was so terrified that I was unable to move. My husband got me out of bed.

What happened to you after that? After my baby girl was born, I began seeing pictures, hearing voices, having dreams at night, and just *knowing*. I've got two guardian angels, my boys, named Raoul and Isaiah, who are still my guides.

All this was not that unnatural for me. The leap to the metaphysical was natural because I have always liked Mother Nature. I used to talk to spiders and ants when I was young.

Describe a typical police case of yours. A trooper phoned me from New Mexico, and I immediately wanted to make the sign of the cross. When that happens, the person is usually no longer in their physical body.

Was the person he was talking about dead? Sure enough, he reported that an unidentified man had been killed near Santa Fe. I opened the Bible, put it on my stomach, and took on the role of the missing man.

How do you do that? Within my own emotional body, I got into his body and became in tune with it. Then I got a feeling like I had to get out; it was hard to breathe. And then everything became light and I was floating, and that's when I saw the picture of what happened. It's as if I have my own built-in antenna, an extra sense that enhances my sight, smell, and touch.

What did you tell the police then? I told the trooper the exact spot along the interstate where the body was found. Then I related to him that the man had picked up hitchhikers, and right after, the car filled up with smoke. The hitchhikers shot the driver, and I gave a general description of the killer.

What was the smoke all about? Following my lead, the authorities located the abandoned car. The smoke I had detected was apparently the result of the two men smoking marijuana together in the car. Roaches, or marijuana cigarette butts, showed up in the ashtray.

How did what you told them lead to the killer? After the police found the car through me, they discovered a bottle for prescription drugs in it—with a label on it containing the name of the killer!

Are you good at getting names of killers? I worked on the brutal murder of an Illinois Bureau of Investigations agent, Peter Lackey. I "saw" him with his neck cut, and he couldn't get away. His arm was shaky, so he couldn't get to his weapon. He had been having trouble with his arm, but he didn't tell anyone for fear of losing his IBI agent position.

I began hearing the name Hanner, Fanner, or Banner. The killer turned out to be named Fanner, and he was nuts and on drugs.

Are the names you come up with usually right? Well, another time, I told the sheriff's department in Des Moines that they would find a woman's body where there was a windmill. They kept looking but couldn't find it. Then they realized that a place they had looked at had a sign saying, Windmill Estates: Property for Sale, and it even had a painting of a windmill on it. The body was there.

What do you like doing best? I do everything from helping senior citizens look for their lost dogs to telling teenagers what the future holds to locating false teeth.

But hand analysis is what brings in the bread and butter. And we need plenty of it because I have nine children from my two marriages plus two Vietnamese boat people my husband and I have sponsored.

How do you do hand analysis? When people come to see me for a reading, I have them prepare an ink print of their hands. I focus on medical issues, love affairs, business, kids having trouble, getting pregnant, and missing people.

Do you do healing? That's a natural focus of my work. Once Debbie Reynolds sent for me to come to Texas to do some healing work for her by using reflexology. I've also worked with Ruth Warrick, Jane Powell, Carrie Fisher, and many others.

You work with death so much. What are your beliefs about the afterlife? When someone has died, I can go into their body and see beyond. Heaven looks like a hallway with many doors. When the main door opens, it looks like forever. It's completely peaceful, and the light is like the sunbeam shining on the earth that you've seen from a plane, only it's whiter, more hypnotic. Angels ascend and descend. It's beautiful there, but it's beautiful here, so it's important to live every day to the maximum.

JIM HECKER

5735 PARK AVENUE
WILMINGTON, NORTH CAROLINA 28403
(910) 392-2909
E-MAIL: JHecker453@aol.com

John Yocum

A bit actor in many movies, he's also a radio personality and a psychic counselor.

When did you realize you were psychic? I remember being psychic since the age of five, but I began to understand that I had divine protection when I was in basic training. I was in the hand grenade pit, learning to throw grenades. The man next to me was freaked out and became so nervous the grenade fell into my slot. Right before it exploded, I felt something and at that moment a voice said, "Leave! Go!" It was so overwhelming that it almost made me go to the bathroom. I reacted and got out of the way. Otherwise, I wouldn't be here today.

How did you get into the movies? About ten years

ago, I met a casting director who asked me if I wanted a part in movies. And I said, "Sure, I could use a couple of days' work." Until then I had been a professional entertainer with a band, but now I've been in many movies—*Teenage Mutant Ninja Turtles, Betsy's Wedding* with Alan Alda.

What are the superstars you've worked with like? Alan Alda was wonderful; we went out and partied. Dustin Hoffman was great. Incidentally, his stand-in in *Billy Bathgate* was a woman! I've worked with Nicole Kidman, Dennis Quaid, and John Goodman. I found Bruce Willis a bit unapproachable.

Is there a relationship for you between movies and the psychic? I consider movies to be motion, vibration, and right brain activity, and the same is true with psychic work, so the two go together for me. Doing movies heightens my awareness for my psychic work by letting me be around artistic people. It's also a break because psychic work does get inundating.

What is the most famous case you've been involved with? The Couch Murder of New Orleans. Two young men and a girl got drunk in a bar one night. All had secret desires to be mercenaries, so they decided to practice a killing.

The woman seduced some guy from the bar and took him to a sleazy part of town. Then the first man strangled him with the cord of a vacuum cleaner. And the other guy hit him with a hammer and then nailed him to a couch before drowning him.

Who were you called in to help? My job was to try to save the second killer from the death penalty. I interviewed him in this little cage—they locked me in with him— and I thought, *Oh, man, here I am with a guy who just murdered someone.*

He was blown away and all he would say was "It's all karma, it's all karma." I tried to talk to him about the crime, but he was out of it, and he didn't make any sense. I meditated on the situation and reenacted the crime in my mind and saw what happened.

What did you see had happened? That he struck

the guy with a hammer, but the guy was already dead. So I said to the public defender, "How can you kill a corpse?" He used that defense in court, and the man avoided the death penalty and got life imprisonment.

Have you been involved in any groundbreaking cases? Yes, one case I worked on was one of the first times DNA [deoxyribonucleic acid] testing was used in a courtroom.

A girl was abducted from a school, taken into the woods, sodomized, and murdered. I went into the pit two days after the crime, and it was pretty gruesome.

What did you "see" there? I saw arteries being opened up and a pink mist surrounding me like I was being sprayed with blood. I could hear her soul crying in grief and misery. Then I saw a flash of blond hair and blue eyes.

Did all this upset you very much? Definitely. That night I got violently ill from experiencing that. I said to the cop, "It's someone close, and he will surface." It turned out it was her boyfriend, and he actually had been at the funeral and put a rose on her coffin. The police incorporated the information I gave them, and it tallied with theirs.

How do you keep in psychic shape? Every morning I do a reading with cards on myself for one hour. I'm spiritually conditioning my psyche the way someone conditions their body.

Do you do psychic work for anyone other than the police? I have a psychic radio show that goes from South Carolina to Virginia. I also do many personal clients. I'm most aware and probably the happiest when I'm doing readings for people.

I have a friend who gave up a PGA golf career to become a spiritual healer. He could have made two hundred fifty thousand dollars a year with blondes on each arm. I can understand why he did it.

ANDREA J. KRAMER

LOS ANGELES, CALIFORNIA
(213) 937-7576

Isabelle M. Basch

*She makes her living doing phone
readings, but she's best known as
a crime psychic, and she received
worldwide publicity when she was
spotted leaving the D.A.'s office right
before the O. J. Simpson trial began.*

What do you call yourself? I don't refer to myself as
a psychic. I'm a clairvoyant, which in Latin means clear-
sighted. I like that term best because the visions I have are
very clear. I sometimes use the alias Claire Voyant.

Were you different from most children? I *felt* that
even before I was five. One problem is that I was secretly
battling dyslexia and fooling everyone. I had a photographic
memory: Someone would read to me, then I would "read"

the same book back out loud, so they thought I was really reading. In the second grade, they saw that I was holding the book upside down and I wasn't really reading at all.

Has your clairvoyance ever helped you person-ally? In my early twenties, I was driving alone at a naval base, and I asked directions from two men in a car who were wearing naval uniforms. They told me to follow them. I started to but had the sense that something was wrong and turned around to get away from them. They then turned around and started following my car.

What happened? I drove away so fast my car hit a tree. It was totaled, but I survived. I later found out these two guys were violent criminals impersonating military officers. God knows what would have happened to me if something hadn't warned me to get away.

Was there a defining moment in your accepting your abilities? That car accident. Until then, I was having a lot of psychic experiences, and I was denying them. But right before my car hit a tree, I heard a voice asking, "Do you want to die?" and I said, "No." And the voice said, "Then you must believe." I think that voice was telling me to accept my intuitions.

How did you get started in police work? I started my professional career in New York City, a happy little copy-writer, introducing Dannon yogurt to California. One day my mother inadvertently left her jewelry in my soap dish, and the jewelry was swiped.

I went into the local precinct, a young girl crying with an empty jewelry box. While I was talking to the detective, I put my hand on a sealed envelope on the desk and started describing the contents of the envelope.

What did you tell them? I gave them a basic descrip-tion of a balding man with a dark-haired girlfriend and said he was going from cold to warm weather. It turned out the contents of the envelope was a dossier sent to all the stations on the Tylenol murders, and my description matched the suspect. The police started inviting me back.

How did you end up working with the LAPD? I hated New York and moved to Los Angeles. I got a parking ticket and went marching to the station. A policeman was walking toward me, and I asked him, "Where's your pin-striped suit? That's your favorite, but I think your wife took it to the cleaners." And then I told him all about his wife and kids. He was impressed and introduced me to other detectives.

Did you have to prove yourself to them? They had me put my hands on a map to look for a body. I'm dyslexic—what do I know from maps? But I put my hand on a spot, and it turned out to be a place where a bone chip had been found. They were intrigued. I found out later this all related to the Billionaire Boys Club case.

Did they test you in any other way? The police also tried to test me by giving me blue books, which are murder books. I described the contents without opening them. One time they gave me the same book twice—they were playing games with me—but I gave them the same details twice.

What was your role in the O. J. Simpson case? I have tried to keep a low profile—this is the first interview I've ever agreed to give—but I was photographed by *Hard Copy* and the *National Enquirer* right before the O. J. Simpson trial started. I was coming out of the office of William Hodgman, one of the early lead prosecutors in the case. After that, the press wouldn't leave me alone. They wrote that I was called in to help the prosecutors look for the knife and hounded me for interviews. I won't confirm or deny anything concerning any ongoing case.

What case are you most proud of? I helped the LAPD get a child rapist a few years ago. He had raped five little girls, some in the back seat of his Cadillac. I gave a description of him and said he would be wearing a blue baseball jacket and blue trousers, that he had a chipped tooth, a limp, something wrong with his mouth, a red post earring, and he would have just had his hair cut.

Did they believe you? One of the policewomen was skeptical, but I kept telling her, "Remember the red. When you see red, you know you have him."

Later, she pulled this guy out of the car, and he's limping like I said, and he's got the chipped tooth like I said, and he's wearing what I said, and his haircut is like I said, and he's got vitiligo on his mouth like I said. And she said her eyes filled with tears because the sun hit his red ruby earring, and all she saw was red. She knew then that she had him.

Why do you choose to work with the police? I do it for the victim and the family. Crime is ugly and it is bloody and it is horrific. If you must get involved and you don't want to be sickened, you have to separate yourself like a surgeon would and do what you can for the victim and their family. If you are doing this for any other motive, you're not coming from a place of God and spirit but from Earth and ego.

Do you also have personal clients? I do private readings and have clients from around the world. I even read someone in Tasmania over the phone. I don't get rich doing individual readings because I go more for quality than quantity. Besides, it's terribly draining so I don't do many cases either.

When you do personal readings, what is your specialty? My forte is names and addresses of people. Locations just come through the air for me; it's a form of telepathy.

I help people who are looking for someone, and I also tell them who they're going to meet. I can do a psychic profile of people and events in their future. Why dwell on what's already happened unless it helps people move on with their lives?

What do you like to do best? I especially like being able to track people. I've helped find kidnapped babies and put together adopted families and missing fathers who have abandoned their children.

JOHN MONTI

POST OFFICE BOX 2323
DUNEDIN, FLORIDA 34697-2323
(813) 734-8767
FAX: (813) 734-4846

He works with prosecutors in high-profile murder and child custody cases.

Why do you call yourself a mentalist instead of a psychic? Years ago we never used the title psychic, which conjures up all kinds of things and opens up the door for Gypsies and that old stuff. Also, I use only my mind—no beads, cards, or anything else.

Was your childhood different? When I was six months old, my mother told me—and it was also in the newspapers—that as she pulled me out of the crib one night there was a bolt of lightning that cut the crib in half like a laser beam. Every fuse in the house melted.

Did this change you? I don't know if that had anything to do with my later abilities, but as a toddler, I could look at people and get impressions.

Any other examples of how you saw things differently after what happened? The only specific thing I can think of is later, when I went to history class, they would be discussing World War II, and I would talk about Vietnam, which hadn't yet occurred. I thought everybody knew what was going to happen beforehand.

Other than that, I had a normal childhood—but *I* was different. That's just the way I was. My father, who was a builder, often took me to work with him to keep an eye on me.

What case that you were involved in got the most publicity? An eleven-year-old girl in New York named Katy Beers disappeared. She had last been seen with a shady-looking family friend name John Esposito. They questioned him and searched his house but couldn't find her or anything to pin on him.

What did you do for her? I saved her life because through me they found her in time. I saw John Esposito on TV crying that he had taken Katy Beers to a video store and lost her. I saw he had something to do with it and that she was being held in a building *under* a house.

I went to see the detectives on the case and told them that Esposito was lying—Katy was under the house. But the detectives said they had looked in the cellar. I said, "No. She's *under* the cellar." They looked at each other like I was crazy. They thought the underground cellar did not exist.

Did you do anything else about it? Yeah, the case really bothered me. I devoted the next twenty-one days to it. I talked to her brother, who indicated that there had been sexual abuse by Esposito. He went public with this information on a special broadcast. Esposito watched the show and then confessed to building a secret underground place where he was hiding Katy—exactly as I had said.

Who else have you located? I worked on the Sidney Russo case, the one where the president of Exxon was kidnapped. I had seen his photo on TV and received impressions that the kidnapper was named Arthur and that he worked as a security guard at Exxon.

I knew that Russo must be rescued soon or he would be dead, that he was being held in a storage warehouse, that he was shot in the hand, and that the wound was becoming infected.

Did you tell anyone about what you saw? I gave the information to a skeptical Long Island publisher, who reported it to the FBI. Soon, they were on top of Arthur Seale, whose testimony in court was word for word what I said.

Have you saved lives in cases that didn't get publicity? A lady once told me she was going to the Caribbean to sit on the beach. She was taking her twelve-year-old son. I told her that when she was on the beach and her son was in the water, she must keep her eyes on him because he would be in danger. I told her to make sure he could swim before they left. I felt pain in my knees when I was discussing this with her.

And what happened? Following my advice, she took the boy to swimming classes before the trip. When she returned from the vacation, she called to tell me she was sitting on the beach and her son was swimming. A guy tried to pick her up. He distracted her for a split-second, just enough time for a motorboat to come along and cut off her son's leg at the knee. The boy swam out of the water carrying his leg. He was not fazed by the incident. When it happened, he said, "Mommy, we just have to get a new leg." He could have been killed. The swimming lessons I suggested saved his life.

NANCY MYER

POST OFFICE BOX 3015
GREENSBURG, PENNSYLVANIA 15601
(412) 832-3951

Sam Gentile

One of America's foremost psychic detectives, she uses psychometry, retrocognition, telepathy, and aura readings to solve crimes.

What can psychics do to convince people of their value? Maybe instead of calling ourselves psychic, we should call ourselves sensitive. I am very sensitive in touch, smell, taste, and hearing. These senses are much more acute in me than in the average person.

Then presumably you don't consider yourself to be average? On the contrary; I've described myself as being disgustingly average. A photographer once asked me to "do something psychic" for a photo. I told him I'd rather not, because I want people to understand that being a psychic is perfectly normal.

When did you realize that you were not entirely what others considered normal? From the time I was a child, I knew that my mind worked differently from others'. I saw and spoke to people no one else could see. I didn't understand how I knew some things and why other people didn't know them also, since they seemed so obvious to me.

Was there anything unusual about your background? My father was in the foreign service and traveled a lot. I had been to twenty-one different schools by the time I got to college. I lived in places like Brazil, Afghanistan, Chile, Ecuador, and Lebanon as a child.

Is that when your psychic abilities came out? It was during my travels that I began seeing the auras around people.

Did you have many friends? I was a lonely child, partly because I was dyslexic and partly because we moved so often that I couldn't make any long-term friends. So I resorted to doing practical jokes on people. For example, with my psychic ability, I knew when they'd be out of the room and I could then shortsheet their beds!

Would you have chosen to be psychic if you could have been otherwise? Being psychic is the last thing I would have wanted to be or thought I'd be, because I thought all psychics were weird. But in my twenties, I started to read about psychic experiences.

Then, one day in 1974, I went into a trance at a Ouija board, and for weeks I was bombarded with the thoughts of everyone I came into contact with. After that, I couldn't pretend to myself that I wasn't different from others.

How did you get involved in police work? The superintendent of the Delaware State Police came to one of my seminars on psychic phenomena. When I was explaining getting impressions about people from objects they owned, he tried to trick me by giving his ring to another trooper to hand to me. But I could sense the ring wasn't the trooper's and spoke directly to Smith.

Was he impressed? He hounded me for months, and I

finally agreed to do a case—just to show him I couldn't do it. But I could!

Were you immediately successful at crime work?
I made some early mistakes. In one case, I described a perpetrator correctly, but I described him as white when he was black. But most of the time I am successful, and these are tough cases, too, because the police don't come to me unless they're really stymied. First they try what's normal, and when that doesn't work, they dump it in my lap.

What makes you good at police work? The police tell me that I am an unusual blend of the psychic and the analytical. It makes it easier for them to work with me because I speak their language.

What do they mean? I'm logical and not off-the-wall. What I look for with my psychic mind is what the cops really want: Who did it and how can we prove it?

I can link my mind with the victim's. It's as if I'm standing alongside him. The victim's brain, even if the person is dead, contains a residue of thought patterns. And I tap into that.

What do you do for the police? In addition to using telepathy to read the thought patterns of victims, witnesses, and killers, I can "read" old photographs to feel what happened at the location of a murder.

I can also see and feel the shape and weight of the murder weapon. I can visualize and sketch the location where a body will be found. I can predict when and where a criminal will strike again.

I run the time clock in my mind back to the date and time of a crime and visualize what happened and where, something called *retrocognition*.

I do remote viewing. I can enter a house and tell you about its former occupants from the thought patterns they have left behind.

Is there anything you can't do well? I get very emotional about cases involving young children, probably because I'm a mother. It's harder for me to be objective in those cases, because my personal feelings interfere with my ability to concentrate.

Do you work well at murder scenes? No, I don't like to go to the murder sites at all. I like best working with photographs. It's usually traumatic for me to go to a murder scene. I get nauseous, and my mind goes blank. I'm filled with so much horror that I temporarily lose my abilities. Once a group of detectives took me to a murder site without telling me. As soon as we walked into the house, I became sick.

What are some of your best-known cases? In 1979, I solved the stabbing death of a woman named Leonetta Schilling in Riviera Beach, Maryland. ·

How? I looked at a stack of photos of thirty-two suspects. I saw that one man's thought pattern was most similar to that of the killer's. I told the police that he knew his victim well.

Who did you think did it? The picture I picked turned out to be that of the victim's nephew, who she once baby-sat for! He was later convicted of murder and sentenced to life in prison.

Give another example of one of your psychic police cases. Another time, I was working on a case and saw that the perpetrator was breathing in a strange way. I saw the man had asthma. There were three suspects in the case, and it turned out the murderer had asthma.

How do you answer critics of crime psychics? I recognize that if you're going to be in this profession, you have to take a lot of flak. My success rate is 80 to 90 percent, and a lot of people find that threatening.

Aren't some of these people critical of all psychics? Yes, many are skeptical of psychics because they mistrust what they can't see or feel and because many people in the field are perceived as frauds. Some people think of psychics as the palm readers along the highway with these little neon signs hung out and fortune-tellers hovering over crystal balls in dark tents.

Have you had to deal personally with many skeptics? I remember at a speaking engagement once when I was attacked by a very rude skeptic. I can read auras and immediately tell when a person is lying because their aura goes gray. I saw from his aura that he was impotent, which gives off a very stressful signal.

Did you say anything to him? I gave him a message only he could understand. He did, and he and his wife later came back to see me, and he apologized to me for his rudeness. But he never understood how I knew what his problem was.

What other kind of psychic work do you do? I have personal clients, and I give them an accurate idea of what is coming up for them in a two-year period. For example, one of my clients was divorced and dating different men for seven years. When she came to me, I told her she'd meet a man from a state south of here in the next two months and marry him within a month.

Did she laugh? She thought I was wrong, but it all took place exactly as I said.

KATHLYN RHEA

34 CARNOUSTIE DRIVE
NOVATO, CALIFORNIA 94949
PHONE AND FAX: (415) 884-2120

A crime psychic who has worked on several major crimes, she teaches law enforcement officers ways to help them solve crimes.

What is your personal background? I was married to a Navy captain. We moved all over the world. I learned what different places looked like and felt like to me. I learned the different feelings associated with a river, the desert, the Gulf Coast.

Did this improve your psychic abilities? I think so, because it helped give me an intuitive exposure that I use when working on a case. I use this knowledge to decipher what certain pictures, sounds, and feelings relate to. For example, I knew that one suspect took his victim into a place with a screen door because I heard the screen door slam.

What is a typical case that you've been involved with? A twenty-two-year-old English girl went to Canada when she realized her visa was expiring. She was probably returning to the States illegally and reentered on foot, traveling through a nonboundary area rather than an official border crossing point. When she was reported missing, they searched the terrain for five days by helicopter but gave up.

What did you do for them? I made a ninety-minute tape from more than one thousand miles away. I put myself into her head and went up the mountain with her. I described the entire area and the girl's walk across the border. I heard a boulder rolling and figured out how long it took until it hit the ground. Then I knew about how high up she was. And I knew she'd be found dead.

Were you on target? Yes, I pinpointed the exact area where she was found. The sheriff was amazed because I correctly described the terrain, the weather, the animals in the area, and what her injuries were.

Have you ever solved a crime and had no one believe you? There was a sensational case in which a woman named Margie Coffey gave up a life of prostitution, became a Jehovah's Witness, and attended college while supporting her two children.

One day her car was found abandoned in Ohio. I was in Maryland, and I was called in on the case. The detective told me he thought she was just hiding out, but I saw that she was dead. I told him where her body was.

Why didn't they believe you? Well, I also saw a uniform and a shiny badge, and told him that a *policeman* had killed her. Furthermore, I told him that the killer had an intimate relationship with the victim and might even be the father of one of her two children.

Did they find her body? The detective took my information, and they found her body a day and a half later. At first his superiors though he might have killed her because he knew so much about the case—of course from me. They thought only someone who had murdered the woman would have known where her body was and everything else. So not only didn't they believe me, they didn't believe *him* at first either.

And were you right about the policeman part?
Yes, they found that this woman had recently filed a paternity suit against a police captain on the same force. He had admitted at one point that he had a love tryst with her and that there was a 99 percent chance that he was the father of her child. When carpet fibers similar to those in his police cruiser were found on her clothes, he was charged with the murder.

Did you ever learn any more about this case?
The officer told a friend who testified against him that she had threatened to go to his wife, and they got into an argument and he killed her. But he claimed to be innocent, and was only sentenced to ten to twenty years in prison.

Have you worked on any well-known cases? In the Polly Klaas case, where someone came right into the house while she had her girlfriends over for a slumber party. He took her away while her mother and younger sister were in bed asleep in the same house.

Who asked you to help on that case? Polly's grandfather came to see me. The investigators had thought the kidnapper was six feet two inches and had a beard and that it was probably a planned revenge crime because of Polly's father or stepfather.

I said he was five feet ten inches and that he *didn't* have a beard, he had a mustache that came down on both sides of his mouth. And I saw that it was a chance thing; he just saw her that evening.

Did you come up with anything else about that crime? Yes, it was so uncanny that I ended up on *A Current Affair* discussing it. I said that the killer had gone out of town on a road beginning with *S* and it ended in a road that had a two in it. And ultimately he was picked up on Highway 12, off of Stonypoint Road, although they didn't arrest him until later. And I said her body would be found in a town that began with *C*, and it was found in Cloverdale,

California. And everything else I had said turned out to be true, and I said it all a month before her body was found.

Have you worked on any mass murder cases? I worked on the Henry Lee Lucas case, the drifter some believe was the worst mass murderer in the country. He confessed to killing three hundred seventy-six people.

I worked with a detective out of San Luis Obispo, where they had found two little girls, five and seven, I think, whom he had raped and killed.

What did you "know" about the killer? I told them the man was no longer in the state, and that he couldn't see out of one eye. I worked with a police artist, and we did several drawings.

When did you find out you were right? Four years later, after they caught Henry Lee Lucas, and he confessed to killing those kids and others, they found that he looked like my drawing—and that he has a glass eye.

What are you best known for? I have been working as a psychic for over thirty years, doing personal and business counseling, although I am best known for my police work.

I also work with attorneys on trial preparation, helping them with their witnesses, enlightening them about the jury, and predicting how the trial will turn out.

I also work with individual families in missing children cases, helping parents get them back in custody cases or finding them if they ran away. Then I work with the child; I try to find out the cause of their troubles and help them to understand themselves.

What do you teach? I have taught courses at several colleges in intuition in law enforcement. I have given a seminar for police from all over the country, The Psychic and Law Enforcement. The purpose is to teach law enforcement people how to use ESP [extrasensory perception] to help solve crimes and how they can form a strong link between hunches and successes.

What change would you like to see in psychic crime work? I would like to see us called in sooner in police cases. By the time I am called, the victim is already deceased.

For example? In one case of a hiker missing in the mountains, I was not consulted until the third day after the forest rangers had been searching unsuccessfully.

Within thirty minutes after they called me, I knew that the team had searched above and below his location. I visualized something yellow nearby. I told them, and they sent in a helicopter again. This time they saw the yellow tag on his backpack. The sad part was that he had been alive for two days but was dead by the time they found him.

Do you consider your work to be dangerous? I own a rottweiler and a loaded .38. I'm deputized, and I've testified in cases. In one instance, I knew that the suspect would kill me if he got loose.

Needless to say, I've asked detectives not to let the criminals know that I was the one who furnished information that helped them get caught.

DAYLE SCHEAR

POST OFFICE BOX 172
ZEPHYR COVE, NEVADA 89448
(702) 588-3337
FAX: (702) 588-5108
E-MAIL: ESP555555@aol.com

Blythe Arakawa

Her specialty is finding missing people using psychometry.

At what age do you think you became psychic?
I believe that I was born a psychic because from the time I was young I wondered if I was. I always knew I was different. I would always pretend.

How did your psychic abilities become apparent?
I may have been the only child to ever dig for buried treasure—and find it. When I was twelve, I dug up about a thousand dollars from the backyard of my parents' luncheonette.

When I told my parents, they discovered that someone was stealing from them. And I was picking up through telepathy where he was burying the money.

What is your most intriguing case? One case that got a lot of publicity was when a dance instructor, Diane Suzuki, disappeared in Hawaii after teaching a class. I lived in Hawaii, and when I searched her studio, I found a pendant, but I didn't know if it belonged to her.

What did you do with the pendant? I asked her family for photos of Diane and found one of her wearing a pendant like the one I discovered. Then I did a reading on the pendant and knew that she had been murdered and had never left the dance studio. I saw that her body was in a swamp nearby. The police didn't believe me. Five years later, they conducted a luminal experiment at the dance studio and found a huge amount of blood exactly where I said it would be. They reclassified the case as a murder.

Which of your cases moved you the most? One of my clients kept hearing the voice of her mother telling her to return to her, but her father said that her mother had died when she was two. In a reading, I held the mother's ring and saw that she was alive living in Germany, waiting for her daughter to find her. I mentioned to the daughter that her mother walked with a limp.

How did your client find her mother? By calling her stepmother and telling her she had been to a psychic who said her real mother was alive. The stepmother believed in psychics, knew the secret was out, and finally told her the truth.

Did the two have a tearful reunion? One month later. And her mother had recently bruised her foot and walked with a limp. My client spent time with her mother, who then died exactly one year after her daughter found her. "Thank you for giving me back my life," the daughter said to me.

How do you think you were able to find her? I believe her mother had unintentionally been sending telepathic signals to her family for help in finding her daughter. I believe our minds have to be receptive for such a linkage to occur. A psychic can see, but it is always up to the individual to pursue the matter. My psychic abilities are almost like a radio wave. It's always on, but I don't hear it until I tune it in.

What is another missing person case that you've handled? I helped locate a ninety-year-old woman who had wandered away from a nursing home. I touched the clothes her daughter brought me and knew her mother was still alive. If she were dead, there would have been no telepathic transmission from her brain. Because I could feel her and visualize her, I knew she was alive somewhere.

Where did you think she was? I said she was near the nursing home, but the police had already searched that area and said she wasn't there. They said it was a residential area and someone would have noticed her if she was actually there.

So what did you do? Her daughter and I went and searched. We found her mother two blocks from the nursing home, still alive. She had been lying for two days in a ditch after wandering away and falling. Her dress had caught on something, so she couldn't get up. She was barely able to speak. She was sending out telepathic signals that she was in danger, and I received those signals.

Have you used psychometry for historical cases? I was called in by the television series *Sightings* to reinvestigate the Lizzie Borden case. I think I was the first person in a hundred years to touch the ax.

Did Ms. Borden take an ax? I believe it was the clinically unbalanced side of her head that did it. I also saw Lizzie trying to poison her father before her mother.

What did you feel at her house? While I was there, I had a feeling of more than just the murder of her parents. Some feeling there scared me so much I wanted to run away.

I found out later that in the house to the right of the Borden house a mother killed her daughters many years ago.

Can you predict things for yourself? Yes, and I love knowing what is going to happen. I am more prepared that way. I can avoid traffic jams or know to spend more time with someone I love who is going to die.

Do you read for yourself? Yes, and when I read tarot cards for myself, I go through the same pain as everyone else. Psychics are not immune from pain; we just have this special gift.

Do you think psychics should tell people the truth even if it's painful? Yes, a good professional psychic will always tell you the truth, not just what you want to hear. While I may turn up things people would rather not see, I am always honest with my clients. I give them their choices and hope they make the right one. The greatest injustice in life is to lead people on. The truth is always the answer.

In your book The Psychic Within, *you give people tips on how to find a good psychic. What are a few ways to tell if one is honest?* You want one who really can see the future and is not just trying to get money from you. I warn people about psychics who say they will remove a curse from you, who ask for more money while they are doing a reading, who tell you evil spirits are lurking around or you are unlucky, or who tell you of your death— all scare tactics for more money.

See: Bertie Marie Catchings, page 45.
        Dorothy Allison, page 281.

CHAPTER

4

Animal Psychics

Christa Carl

486 OCEAN AVENUE
BROOKLYN, NEW YORK 11235
(718) 769-9064

Harold Egeln, Jr.

An animal psychic, she is most famous for being called in to find Tabitha, the cat who disappeared on a Tower Air flight.

How did you get involved in this famous lost animal case? I was called in by the Animal League a few days after Tabitha, a striped tabby, disappeared during a flight on Tower Air from New York to Los Angeles. Her owner got off the plane, but Tabitha didn't. She remained hidden in the plane for twelve days while it traveled thirty thousand miles from New York to Los Angeles to San Juan to Miami again and again.

Did you work on finding Tabitha before you actually got on the plane? Yes, I worked at home every day with Tabitha for about five or six days, about thirty to forty minutes each session. I was communicating with her all the time to help her find food and water so she could stay alive in the plane. I fed her with energy and let her talk to me about what was going on in her life and some of the issues that were upsetting her. We worked on one of her past lives to see how that was connected to her not coming out.

How did this help? I brought her into the light—animals have to come from the darkness into the light—with visualizations. After each session, she was able to release some of her negativity and moved closer to the light as she became more aware of herself and her problems. What she basically did was soul-searching, this cat.

What did you do once you got on the plane? After the airline got a lot of bad publicity and was threatened with a lawsuit, they finally grounded the plane, and we got on it from midnight to eight so we could look for her. I started off with a prayer. I asked God, my spirit guides of the light, and the goddesses of the animal kingdom to help this animal to come out. I asked them if Tabitha was still there and alive and if it would pay to work on her. They told me she was alive and still in the plane. Then my spirit guides told me exactly which seat to sit in.

How did you get Tabitha out? I lit a candle, and I started working with her. My energy went through her energy, and I visualized putting magnets on her and magnets on me and magnets on her owner, so we could all help pull her out.

I also checked a map of the inside of the plane with a pendulum, and I checked my guides and saw from both that she was moving from the wing toward the cargo area and coming out. Then I literally went through the walkways with her, with visualization, going through all the doorways, showing her how to come out because we couldn't get in to pull her out. There are very few openings inside a plane, and the opening where she was, was too small.

And what happened? I guided the search team to the drop ceiling where she was hiding. She was exactly where I said she'd be. Then we heard her come to one of the openings we had created because we had opened all the bins so she could come out.

Was it very emotional? When her owner heard her cry and knew she was alive, she cried. Everybody cried. Tabitha was safe.

Do you find lost dogs, too? I've just finished working on a lost dog. The dog told me last night he feels all the upsets at home and that's why he disappeared. I haven't found exactly where he is yet, but I generally ask animals to send me pictures of where they are and their surroundings, and that is how they will be found.

How do you do visualizations with lost animals? I lay out a map and my spirit guides come through a pendulum that I use to tell me where to look for them: what state they're in, what county. And then I zero in. I communicate with my spirit guides and telepathically with the pet at the same time. Sometimes guides give me names and clues.

Do you always get your pet? No, I saw that one dog was sold to a lab somewhere out in New Jersey and that he was being experimented on for AIDS and cancer. The owners and I decided to let him go; the guides said it was too late, that we were not going to be able to get him, and he was too weak and would not make it.

Do all lost animals want to come back? When I reach a lost animal, I have to ask him if he wants to come home, and I have to respect the animal's wishes.

If they do want to come home, then through visualization, I literally put out a path for them to find their way home. I connect the pet with his home. I put a white carpet on the floor and candles around the owner's house so they can find their way. But some animals still don't want to come home, and then you have to let them go because it's their choice if they're not being physically restrained.

Do you do any work with animals other than finding them? I talk to birds. I've done a couple of lizards. They don't differ from primates at all. The two lizards I went to see were concerned about food. They were able to tell me to tell their owner they didn't want to eat eggs. It was making them sick.

What about horses? I work with a lot of horses. Today, a friend of mine who is a mounted police officer called me, and it just came to me that his horse, Sterling, was depressed and sad.

Animals have just as much emotion as we have. Anyone can tune into their animals if they take the time. Just ask your animals, "What is going on?"

Do you communicate with animals who are no longer with us? I have séance readings for animals who have already passed over. They have unfinished business down here. I bring them together with the people who lost them.

Give an example of a séance with a dog. Brandy, a dog, had been placed in a kennel by her owner when she got married. She broke away from the kennel and got killed.

Her owner called me and told me she was having a hard time and wanted to communicate with Brandy. When I did the reading with Brandy, I learned from her that she didn't know why she had been put in the kennel. She had felt abandoned, unloved, uncared for.

Her owner should have told her ahead of time why she needed to put her in a kennel. I explained it to Brandy, and now she's at peace.

What should people do to ensure they are always with their pets? You can make agreements now with your animal to have them come back in the form of another animal in another life. I've talked to animals who want to come back to the same person. I recommend that people make these agreements with their pets before they die.

When did your psychic abilities come out? It started three years ago when I moved into a new house that had a gas leak and I got terribly sick. I had seizures and breathing problems. The gas leak caused chemical imbalances in my body.

What did you do about these problems? I spent two years in and out of hospitals trying to figure out what was wrong with me. I had to quit schools and jobs. I couldn't get myself around or take care of myself. Doctors couldn't give me any answers.

Before my accident, I was working full-time, twelve to fourteen hours a day, as a manager with the Circle Line, a sight-seeing company in New York. But my body just came to a halt.

Did a psychic help you? That's right. I had never been psychic before, but a year and a half ago. I found a spiritual counselor who helped to put me on my road, to deal with my emotions, to work on my self-esteem.

But when did you become a psychic? At the same time I was seeing this psychic, my girlfriend told me about a group involved in channeling with spirits. I told her I thought those people must be off base. But I started having sessions with one of the teachers. He taught me what I could do to help myself, and I started to heal. And then I started working on pets.

Do you work alone? I have a family of spirit guides. The main guides oversee my entire life and have introduced me to other guides. They appear to me to be people who wear different-colored clothing. Each one speaks differently. Like people, they have different personalities. Some are gentle, some are more male, some are more female.

KAREN HAMEL-NOBLE

ROUTE 6, BOX 210
STILLWATER, OKLAHOMA 74074
(405) 377-2668

Anthony Hart

*This equine parapsychologist
specializes in healing horses.*

Do you own horses? Yes. I live in Stillwater, Oklahoma,
with my husband, Lenn, and we raise registered quarter
horses, and Lenn trains futurity barrel horses, team horses,
and steer-roping horses. With everything that happens training horses, my abilities to read and heal the animal are put
to use every day.

Do you know when a horse will not make it?
Toward the end, I can see it in their energy field. Remember
the story of Edgar Cayce and the elevator? He had been in a
department store, looking at red sweaters. When the elevator
doors opened, he realized the people inside had no color
around them, meaning their energy was gone. So he didn't

get on the elevator, which crashed to the basement, killing all aboard. When your time is up, the energy leaves naturally.

Give an example of a horse who has lost its energy field. I was doing some metaphysical checks—meaning without their physical presence—for some Texas horses, using stacks of registration papers. While going through the papers of one horse, I had trouble getting energy. I couldn't understand why.

I went to see her, and she looked fine. Later, I did another reading on her back home and got no energy at all. I went out to the field and discovered she had died.

How did you get interested in horses? I was brought up on a ranch in Idaho, which brought me eye to eye with Mother Nature. We had baby colts and puppies. My sister and I spoiled the animals rotten, dressing the puppies in doll clothes and such.

Describe your healing ability with horses. I had no idea that I had this gift until I started doing it. I was working with sick horses and didn't know what I could do to help them. When something was unbalanced in a horse, I began looking at its energy field. A horse can look good on the outside—healthy and shiny—but be screaming on the inside.

Specifically, how did you heal them? I started holding my hands over their bodies and spotting the source of weakness in their energy fields. Then I allowed the animal to take as much energy from me as it needed.

What happened the first time you tried it? The first time I healed a horse she had been cut badly, probably from rolling into a barbed-wire fence. The mare was standing on three legs. I knew the affected part of the leg could not be sewn because it looked as if it had gone through a shredder. When she tried to move, the sound coming from the gaping cut was like a loud sucking noise.

Did you automatically know what to do? I had absolutely *no* idea what to do. I suggested that the owner call a vet, but she trusted us. I was doing readings then on horses, and the thought that came began as a recipe: Mix half apple cider vinegar and half water and spray it on the wound. Then came the instruction to place black table pepper on the wound and give the horse a penicillin shot. I knew apple cider vinegar was a tremendous fighter against infection. I also knew that black pepper tends to heal wounds from the inside out.

Did it work? I applied the recipe and did hands-on healing, and she took the energy through me. Within three weeks, she was healing beautifully, and her leg didn't make that awful sound when she walked. After three months, you had to get on your knees to see the scar. It had healed perfectly. I was impressed.

Amelia Kinkade

WEST HOLLYWOOD, CALIFORNIA
(818) 766-4344

Photography by Michael Helms

This former jazz dancer is now an animal psychic who teaches courses in how to communicate telepathically with your pet.

How do you communicate with animals? In person, over the phone, or through photos sent by mail.

What do they tell you? Animals give me lots of information, including some regarding their owners. They describe fights in the family. They're often funny because animals have a wonderful sense of humor. They overhear phone conversations. They give names and numbers. They tell me that they like some people better than others.

Give an example of something a pet told you. One dog I worked with complained to me that he liked someone he used to know better than he did his current friends. He described a tall, silver-haired man. The owner knew who I was talking about. It was the vet who cared for the dog years earlier.

What type of animal problems do you handle? Dogs that are becoming vicious, horses that won't jump, lizards that won't move, or cats that won't behave.

What causes these problems? Some of them come from present conditions. Some come from past lives. Some come from past *owners*. For example, when people get animals from shelters, they often arrive with phobias from prior families.

What mistakes do people make when dealing with animals? They see in their minds what they do not want to happen. They will say to their dog, "Don't bite," and they see a picture of a dog biting. They will be visualizing what they fear.

What should they be doing? We should always be working in the affirmative. Tell the dog, "Keep your teeth in your mouth," or "Keep your jaw shut."

If an animal is sick, they shouldn't be thinking about the illness. To heal a sick animal faster, people should see the animal well and keep repeating the message to get better.

Can people make animals sick? Yes, especially because of stress. There is often a correlation between people's lives and their pets' illnesses because animals are like sponges. They soak up what's occurring at home.

An example, please. I wanted to know why a German shepherd had a cyst. He told me that he went to the office every day with a man he called his father, who was his owner. He was a high-powered successful salesman, and the dog told me his father was having problems with a man the dog felt was dangerous. The dog was upset and agitated. This in turn lowered his immune system.

Were you able to confirm this? Yes, from the owner, who told me that his business partner was volatile, and they were having major problems and numerous arguments.

Do cats also get problems from their owners?

That often happens. One cat was constantly throwing up. When I asked the cat about this, it told me, "It's not good to keep food in your system." I asked the owner, "Are you dieting?" She was. If an owner is projecting that he or she can't eat, the animal won't eat either.

Do you work with animals who are deceased? I talk to them as much as live animals. Our departed pets spend some time on the other side—usually with one of our deceased relatives who is an animal lover—and some time reincarnated back to us.

When does the animal come back? How quickly they return here after they die is up to them. Usually, after a long illness, they want time on the other side. Those killed instantly come back the quickest.

Do you think everyone can communicate psychically with their pets? Yes, everybody is born with some psychic ability. Children use it until they go to school. But when children say something, parents always say, "No, no, no, it's not true," and they lose some of their abilities.

Still, when we grow up, we communicate with our pets more than we realize. For example, in this class that I teach, we did an experiment with two German shepherds, making them guinea pigs, if you'll pardon the expression.

How did you teach the students to communicate with the shepherds? The owner of the German shepherds dressed them up each year for Christmas cards. The students had to guess what their outfits were without seeing the cards. They had to just ask the dogs what they wore each Christmas and what their favorite outfits were.

Did it work? Absolutely. Everyone got information from the dogs. They correctly guessed that one year the dogs wore leather jackets and were bikers, and another year they were in Tahitian costumes. So people already communicate with their animals telepathically more than they realize.

PENELOPE SMITH

PEGASUS PUBLICATIONS
POST OFFICE BOX 1060
POINT REYES, CALIFORNIA 94956
(415) 663-1247
FAX: (415) 663-8260

© 1993 Marty Knapp, Point Reyes, CA

She is an animal psychic known for her lectures, books, and audiotapes on interspecies telepathic communication.

What is an outstanding animal memory from your childhood? Our family had a parade of animal companions when I was young—goldfish, turtles, parakeets, cats, and dogs. My closest animal friend was Winky, a blue parakeet, who would perch on my glasses and preen my eyelashes and eyebrows.

What happened with Winky? When I was about eleven years old, he bit me hard on the nose. In shock and pain, I struck out at him, and he was slammed against the wall.

Soon afterward, he began to have seizures. The vet gave him medication and my parents charged me an enormous amount of my allowance, but it didn't help. Winky never forgave me. I knew the seizures were the result of our upset.

My older brother agreed to take Winky to his home to care for him. He never had another seizure and lived happily for many years with my brother.

When did you realize you could communicate with animals? As a very young girl, I knew that animals were intelligent beings who could understand each other and could understand people and that we were alike except for physical appearance. When other children made fun of my communication with animals, I learned to keep these wonderful experiences to myself.

Give an example of your own telepathic interspecies communication. In 1976, I first met llamas while visiting the Los Angeles zoo. I asked the three llamas if they would come out to visit with me. They shied away so I sang to them. Then I danced for them. Soon, the leader came running in my direction and accompanied me in the dance back and forth beside the fence. The others tried to join in, but she warned them back, saying, "This is for me alone." Fifteen years later, I acquired my own llamas when Regalo and Raindance joined my family.

Is it hard to communicate with animals? Communication with animals is just like a conversation with another person. Most animals, if you are honest, will respond to you. They're usually overjoyed to meet a human being who communicates through thoughts and feelings instead of just observing their behavior. They're very good at picking up emotions, especially strong ones. Love enhances telepathy, which is a universal language.

How can people do it? To communicate with animals, you need to believe in your own intuitive ability to give and receive telepathic communication. You must be receptive and listen to anyone of whatever species.

You have to slow down and tune in, and then you may find yourself much more aware of the nature of life around you. This requires a quiet attention, a calmness that many humans in our industrialized, commercialized cities and revved-up lifestyles have long ago lost.

Can one communicate with potentially dangerous animals? While hiking through the hills of California with my dogs, I heard a loud rattle. There was a coiled-up rattlesnake, ready to strike. I respectfully asked if he would uncoil and go the other way. The snake took off in the other direction.

What types of cases have you commonly handled? One woman's normally affectionate cat started running to the top of the refrigerator whenever she came home. When I asked the cat what was going on, he told me that his owner had stopped going to her meditation class. Because the cat knew that meditation was helping his owner grow spiritually, he was withholding affection to get her to go back.

What happened then? I asked the owner about this, and she admitted she wasn't going to her classes. When she agreed to go back to class, the cat came down off the refrigerator, jumped in my lap to thank me, and went to his owner.

Do you commonly work with cats? I am often called upon to help when cats pee or spray outside their litter box. For example, Dixon was a three-year-old neutered male who had been spraying around the house for a few months, destroying furniture and carpeting.

   Communicating at a distance, Dixon showed me images of a strange wild dog coming to the sliding glass doors of the home when his people were away. Dixon sprayed in the house as a signal that this was his and his family's territory. It also relieved the tension and fear he felt upon seeing the predator.

Were you able to find out if Dixon was telling you the truth? His people confirmed that coyotes had been spotted in the neighborhood. I suggested that the owners acknowledge Dixon's good intentions and also patrol for coyotes before leaving for work in the morning. Dixon was greatly relieved.

Is there any animal you feel particularly close to? I have always had a special affinity for whales. They are the ancient guardians, the wise ones of the sea. I believe that without their presence on earth, ecological balance and harmony would be destroyed.

Did you try to communicate telepathically with them? When someone wrote to me requesting that I do something about the decimation of the whales, I communicated with the whales.

They told me that they felt their time had come to leave the earth, that reaching humans was beyond hope now, that humans continued to slaughter them and the rest of the earth's animal population. The whales and I conversed, communed, and prayed together.

Did you do something else? I performed my special psychic dance and promised to dedicate future dances in their honor. As I danced and prayed, I felt their connection and decision to regroup, repopulate, and return. They understood the plight of the humans and have renewed their pledge to help.

How important are animals to you? I wouldn't live in an artificial environment with a barren earth just to stay physically alive. My very being and purpose is linked with other beings. My work with humans would not be possible without the support and power of animals and other species.

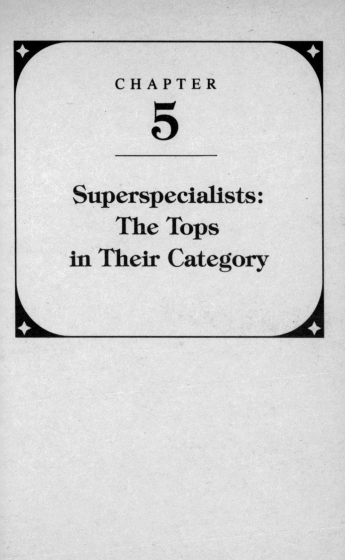

CHAPTER

5

Superspecialists:
The Tops
in Their Category

KIM ALLEN

1438 FULTON STREET, APT. 144
BROOKLYN, NEW YORK 11216
(718) 622-1402
E-MAIL: KAllenSeer@aol.com

Devon Cass

She's so good with tarot cards, she can read four decks at once.

How does your gift affect your private life? My husbands hated to think in my presence because I would pick up their thoughts.

In my last relationship, I used to tell my boyfriend things about his brother. I knew he was up to no good, although I hadn't met him. When I turned out to be right, my boyfriend got suspicious and thought maybe I knew so much about his brother because I was interested in him!

When did your talent reveal itself? When I was a little girl, I used to travel astrally at night. I would just float around. I found myself places. When I got up in the morning, I was always very tired.

Do you remember any places you went to? Yes, my parents' bedroom! One night, when I was just a little bitty girl, I floated around into my mother and father's room, and they were making love. It sort of startled me. I stopped floating then until I was thirteen. I was relieved to finally lie down, without flying all over the place.

Is your psychic ability always turned on? I have friends who are clairvoyant, and a lot of them are in and out of the nuthouse because they're always "tuned in." I have clairvoyant friends who are constantly connected with their dead ancestors, and they can't turn off certain things. When I pick up the tarot cards, it allows me to "turn it on" when I need it, to control when I want to use my gift.

Have you ever used your psychic abilities in unusual ways? I'm a very free-spirited person, and before I knew how to use my gift, I would torture my supervisors. I was working as an administrative assistant for the Metropolitan Museum of Art, and after a few weeks, I tuned into my bosses' thoughts. I would find out which pens were their favorites and what things aggravated them the most, and I would sabotage them, because I have a thing with authority.

How does your talent work? I know everything as soon as people sit down. They are often angry when they walk out. I have this big police stick sitting next to my desk just in case I am attacked!

Do you always tell them the truth? I tend to be very truthful. They come back six months later and say, "I hated you the first time I sat down with you. But everything you say is the truth and is manifested!"

People have a very hard time accepting the truth. I tell them, "Don't come to me unless you want to know the truth. I am not going to tell you lies. That's not why the Lord has put me into this business."

What is the most outrageous example you can think of? A West Indian woman came to me. She lived in Brooklyn. I kept telling her, "Your husband is married to another woman." She laughed at me. Six months later, she told me that he did have another wife in New Jersey. I told this woman to let her husband go. "I'm the wife!" she said.

Neither wife would turn him in because both of them were afraid that the other one would then have him.

How did you know about the other wife? It was the cards that told me. I've done this so long, you just have to trust what comes to you or you're in the wrong field.

Can you read everybody? There are very few people I cannot read. If I can't, then maybe it is not time for them to know certain things. They have put up a wall of resistance. Maybe their spirit guide does not like my spirit guide.

What do your friends think about your being a professional psychic? For a long time I didn't tell my friends I was doing this. I was already labeled as odd and strange. This is the last thing that I wanted held over my head.

Do you ever give free readings? Sometimes people come into my shop who can't pay their rent. I give them a reading free and tell them to get themselves together.

What is your method for reading tarot cards? Anybody can get a book and interpret the cards. But an artist sees things differently. It's the difference between painting-by-the-numbers where the scene is not moving and has no depth to it and having an artist who has the gift do the same scene. It comes alive; I'm an artist rather than a technician.

Was there a book that helped you learn how to do it? Tarot cards reinterpret themselves to you, so training from a book doesn't help. Many different tarot readers will give you different readings for the same display of cards. Tarot is a gift. I can read four decks at once. I'm a Virgo. I tend to digest information quickly.

Do you have spirit guides? I have three spirit guides who whisper things in my ears. I can see "ethereal fingers" that point certain tarot cards out to me. Sometimes I can see something growing out of the cards.

Give an example of something you've seen in the cards. Recently, during a reading for a man, I saw him pumping weights. And he said he had just started lifting weights two days earlier!

How can one recognize a genuine tarot reader from a phony? There are a lot of bunco artists in the field of tarot reading. I do not believe in curses. I believe in changing the destiny from within, trying to change the way people see things.

In the African-American community, we have always had our readers. We just didn't talk about it. A true reader must keep his or her heart and mind pure. You cannot do this work and drink. You cannot let in negative spirits. I'm better when I'm rested. I work three or four days a week only.

It is easy for a bad psychic to take advantage of people. People come to a psychic in a very unprotected state. But it's a sin to take advantage of a person when he or she is vulnerable.

ANABEL

QUEENS, NEW YORK
(718) 631-2142

Terry Chenaille

*She does aura portraits and determines
people's personalities and their futures
by the aura that surrounds them.*

What is your specialty? As a psychic, my unique talent
is in aura portraits. The aura is the energy field around the
body, and it consists of a variety of colors. I create portraits
using color from the energy field.

Do you paint an aura around the entire person?
I work only with the face. I see an assortment of colors
around it, which I paint, and then I do the reading based on
the colors that come through.

Does this help people? With the application of color, I
can help to heal any emotional imbalances. Anger, mistrust,

and disappointment can be transformed into peacefulness, trust, and fulfillment.

I also guide people into past lives if necessary and explain what gifts and talents they've brought into their present lives. But I only do it if I'm invited in. Otherwise it's an invasion of privacy.

Can you give an example of what you do for your clients? If I'm making an aura portrait and red appears around the person's face, it could represent anger or energy that isn't being used. I tell the people what I see and advise them to meditate on the colors that are in the aura portrait because usually they're there to help them. Meditating on those colors permeates their inner beings and helps ease them out of the situations they're in.

Do certain colors mean something? Yes, for example, blue corresponds to resistance or stubbornness. Pink may show that these people have new beginnings or new events, a possible pregnancy, or a new way of life or a sense of self. Orange represents ambition and pride.

Were you an artist or a psychic first? Maybe both. When I was two years old, I was sitting on the floor in the kitchen with my parents. I saw pictures in the marbleized linoleum. My father told my mother, "She's either going to become a psychic or an artist." I am now both.

What kind of work did you do before doing aura portraits? At one time I was a textile designer. My work looks Old World, like the Victorian era. Once I did a design of black-and-white butterflies and roses for a dress for Diana Ross that became a commercial design.

I've spent thirty years painting watercolors and pastels. I've displayed my work in many galleries, had an outdoor show, accumulated twenty-five awards, and have illustrated the covers of New Age books, and I teach.

Jeannine Parvati Baker

POST OFFICE BOX 398
MONROE, UTAH 84754
(801) 326-4256

Photo by Sue Coleman

*She specializes in helping pregnant
women to communicate psychically
with their unborn children.*

**How can women tune into their children before
they're even born?** I counsel a mother to *listen* to the
soul of her child so she can get into psychic communication
with her unborn child during pregnancy. Mothers are already
in *physical* communication because there is a chemical dialogue occurring between the two, a hormonal interplay between mother and fetus.

Will this come as a surprise to most mothers?
Mothers have always known they can communicate with
their baby. I encourage women to make conscious what already exists. The more awareness a woman brings to the

creative dialogue she is already in, the better able she is to be a partner with the baby in its birth.

Concretely, how can they get in touch with their child? If a woman can conceive a baby, she can talk with it. I suggest that women enter into an imaginal dialogue with their prebaby through journal writings or spontaneous discussions. The mother should invite the voice of the pre-baby to enter, and she should converse with that soul.

Why should women communicate with their unborn child? Babies have important information, and they can give us practical information, like how we can eat, exercise, and optimally prepare ourselves for the great work of being a mother, and a father—fathers can participate as well.

What should a mother do when she realizes she is pregnant? As soon as you know you have conceived a baby, close your eyes and take a moment or two to inhale and exhale. Then place your hand over your heart and inhale slowly. As you breathe in, bathe that baby with the love that brought him or her here. Next, place your other hand on your abdomen, and as you inhale, wash your baby with love. As you exhale, clear your mind. You can do this over and over again with slight modifications.

What are these modifications? For example, as you inhale, ask your baby a question like, How may I serve you? And then listen to the response as you exhale.

Do you believe women can psychically tune into their children even before they're conceived? I know I can tune into that soul before the conception occurs, and I can enter an imaginal dialogue with my prebaby then. I can ask my pre-baby how I can prepare for him or her and how I can serve him or her.

If there is anything I've learned through having six children, it is that to be my children's servant in a respectful relationship starting with conception strengthens the maternal experience.

This is pretty radical. What do you base preconception psychic communication on? As well as being a midwife, I'm a perinatal psychologist. I believe the soul is present at the moment of conception. When two people come together and fall in love, it's not just a conspiracy of chromosomes that brings them this specific soul, their child. The great mystery is where that soul is just before conception.

Can you help women with difficult pregnancies?
Yes, and I don't even have to be with them. I'm assisting a woman now who is going to have her baby soon. She was bleeding, and a miscarriage was threatened.

How did you help her without being with her?
After counseling her by phone, I asked my spirit to assist, and while I meditated, I got a clear picture of what was wrong with her. In my next phone call, I shared my vision with her. It was an image not of a baby in distress but of a primal wound.

What was that from? It had to do with adultery. Her husband had just come back from Europe, and I saw an image of him with another woman. I shared that with her. She confronted her husband with that. He confessed. She stopped bleeding.

Do you often help women through birth without being there? Yes, I can show up at times of birth even though I'm not physically there. People tell me afterward that I was there, and they send me checks in the mail! It's a cost-effective way to run a practice because I haven't left my own home!

I sometimes have a corresponding *dream* of being at the birth the same night as the birth occurs. It's beyond the realm of coincidence—I am there psychically.

Could there be any explanation for why this works other than a psychic one? One rational explanation of this is that people have heard or seen me on radio and television. My words stay with them, and the women become their own midwives.

Do you encourage women to give birth at home?
I became involved with birth experientially by delivering my first baby myself. I am against women having their babies at hospitals if there is nothing wrong with the mother or child.

I believe that if you can conceive a baby without experts,

you can birth a baby without experts, too. You don't need them at the conception and you don't need them at the birth.

Why? Birth has been medicalized and should instead be ecstasy. It's trickier for some couples to experience sexual ecstasy giving birth when they're surrounded by masked men, whom I call paid paranoids.

Were you brought up in a psychic home? I wisely chose my parents. My mother is a psychic; she calls it "the knack." The phone rings and she knows who is calling.

My father is Native American, born on a reservation in Washington State. He inherited a world view that is aware of the subtle influences we pick up in addition to what the five senses tell us.

And your husband? He's psychic, too. He's a visionary. He works here helping the Payute Indians and leading family vision quests into the wilderness.

Are your children psychic? Five of my children were born at home, and the last three of my six children were born without medical assistance and two of them in free birth, underwater. Those two especially seem to show unparalleled psychic capacities compared to those in "dry birth."

Can you give us an illustration of this? One of these boys, when he was five, announced that our missing cat had been shot. We later found the cat with a bullet in it.

Do you have grandchildren? Not yet, but they will be psychic. I'm now dreaming of future grandchildren. I've seen some of their faces already. It will be a reunion because, in one sense, I already do know them.

How is that possible? When I carried my daughters, they had eggs in development, which are my grandchildren. As women, we are all born with the genetic material of all of our children and our grandchildren already in us. We carry the continuum of life in us.

Clarisa Bernhardt

(818) 906-6767
FAX: (204) 956-4987

Photo by Norm Levi

The "Earthquake Lady" predicts earthquakes and hurricanes and knows how to prevent them.

Where does your psychic talent come from? When people ask where I get my information from, I say it comes from the "Universal Broadcasting System." Actually, my mother was a full-blooded Cherokee, and my grandfather was chief of one of the smaller tribes. I attribute part of my intuitiveness to my Cherokee side because the Indians, more than people in some other cultures, had to use their sixth sense for survival.

Were you psychic as a child? Ever since I was a child, I have always had the ability to see the lights around people, which some call the aura but I know is the magnetic field. As a little girl, I noticed that the lights would change around people. If someone was well, they would be very bright and pretty, but if the person was angry or sick, they were dark. And I always thought everyone else saw it like I did.

Did others know of your abilities early on? I learned when I was young that not everyone I met shared my enthusiasm or ability. So I kept quiet about it. Although my family and friends knew I had the talent, I never really felt any practical need to use it, except that I always knew what was in the Christmas packages before I opened them. In fact, my family used to think I had peeked at them in advance.

When did you start predicting earthquakes? I was attuned to the weather as a child, but I kept quiet about that, too. When I was a young woman, I taught Sunday school but was fired when I said I believed in reincarnation.

I ended up in Hollywood doing public relations. It was when I moved to California that I realized I had the ability to predict earthquakes.

What was your first earthquake prediction? I had a radio show in Los Gatos, and I interviewed scientists, lawyers, and people from everyday life who used their sixth sense in their work. In 1974 I asked a friend, "Do you think it's OK for me to predict an earthquake on my show? Because there is going to be an earthquake on Thanksgiving Day." He said, "Go ahead. If it doesn't happen, no one will remember it." So on my show I announced, "If you don't want your turkey to slide across the table, wait until after three for the meal because there's going to be an earthquake right after three o'clock."

And what time was the earthquake? At 3:01 to the minute, and my life was never the same after that. My prediction was put into several newspapers. The press rushed in because they felt if you can predict one earthquake, you can predict another.

Are you still this accurate? My visions are always 100 percent accurate. I can see earthquakes a day or years in advance. The U.S. Geological Survey contacted me in 1975 and asked if I would take part in a study. And at the end of the project I beat two hundred scientists, other psychics, dreamers, regular people, and a computer in predicting earthquakes.

In what form do you see your vision of the quake? I see a calendar with a circle and the word *earthquake* on the date and then the number for the magnitude of the quake. Sometimes I also get very confused and disoriented before an earthquake.

Do you like predicting earthquakes? Yes, because I feel they are an excellent demonstration of the sixth sense because they are so documentable. You can put something in print before it happens and prove afterward that something did happen.

Do you only predict earthquakes? No. I predicted Hurricane Andrew in the newspapers, and I said it would be the worst hurricane in Florida's history. And then it happened.

Do you apply your sixth sense to other phenomena? Yes. I use it myself. I believe that your life is a lot better if you use your sixth sense because it can help you avoid accidents and bad business decisions. Being psychic is also fabulous for finding parking spaces. It's always fun when my husband says, "Find us a parking place," and one opens up.

Is there any downside to this? A problem is that people who know that we're applying our sixth sense to things think we're *always* doing it. I find people thinking that I know everything about them. They'll say, "I know you probably already know this about me; please don't tell my husband."

What other type of psychic work do you do? I have also done volunteer work with a search and rescue unit in California, although I do less now because there's so much pain around someone who is missing and I've become too sensitive over the years to pain.

Can you cite an instance of someone you've found? There was a young man who was missing, and his mother came to me and asked me if I could help her find him. By touching his photo and some keys that belonged to him, I sensed that he was going to be at his father's house.

When I told his mother, she said, "That's impossible. I've been divorced from his father and he hasn't seen him in ten years."

Did she check anyway? Reluctantly, she went over to the father's house, and while she was there, the boy arrived. And this so upset the boy. "How did you know I was going to be there when I didn't know I was going to be there myself?" he asked me.

Can you give another illustration of your ability to find people? A woman had been missing for three weeks when her husband came to me. I touched her rings and helped him find her. I thought I had done something wonderful.

But two to three weeks after this, she called me and said, "I'm getting ready to get lost again. *Don't find me.*" Then I had to do some soul-searching because I wondered, "Am I interfering with a person's free will?" If it was a child, I would have helped him again, but she was an adult and could make up her own mind.

So what did you do? I decided she had a right to get lost. So this time I didn't look for her even though her husband used to call me all the time and say, "I've had reports that she was here or there." I don't think she was ever found.

How can people be affected by other people's thoughts? Magnetic field thoughts are very powerful. You can feel these forces when you walk into a room and feel comfortable or uncomfortable with a group of people. You're feeling the vibrations these people radiate so you stay or you say, "I can't stand these people," and bug out.

Can each person's thoughts make a difference? Thoughts are forces. You hear people clap and then stop, and you see the sound waves go soft. Just as you would feel toward a puppy or kitten or a sunrise, so you can send a beautiful thought, a nice feeling, radiating.

Every person has to be a little more responsible for their thoughts. Science is going to discover soon that the thought energy that emanates from individual thoughts also creates energy changes and contributes to weather changes and earthquakes.

Can we actually prevent earthquakes? Where there's a sensitive part of the earth, when one group is tossing hate out at the other, earthquakes can happen. That big earthquake happened in the San Fernando Valley, which is exactly where those guys were tried for beating up Rodney King.

If people expect certain things, they will attract it to themselves. So let's all be responsible for our thoughts and send love to the planet because bad things don't have to happen.

Everybody should be prepared and make sure all the physical needs are taken care of if there's an earthquake or a hurricane. But if you want to stop these disasters altogether, you have to start sending love and loving thoughts to the planet.

How? You can hold up your hand in front of a map and aim it toward some area and say, "I send love and peace to the planet." Now that would just be one person doing it. But if everybody does it, it makes a difference.

KENNETH DICKKERSON

215 WEST 104th STREET, BOX 0165
NEW YORK, NEW YORK 10025
PHONE AND FAX: (212) 222-1003
E-MAIL: gibson@interport.net

He is a lottery psychic who not only has helped his clients but also has won many times himself using his psychic system.

How often have you won the lottery? Many, many times. My last big win was last year; when I won $15,800 on a four-digit combination purchased for five dollars. Another year I won the lottery 246 times—it was easy. Not only do I play Pick 3 or Pick 4, but also Pick 5, 6, and 10. I play all those games.

How did you get started? I always thought I would be good at playing numbers, but I didn't do it because my parents were not numbers players. I think I was always psychic, but I didn't know it. Then one day, when I was almost asleep, lying in the twilight zone, the number nine floated past my inner vision. Then a seven. And I said to myself, "Where is the third number?" Then a three floated by.

What did you do about this? I told myself I would play the numbers for three days. I played that day, Friday. I didn't win. Saturday, no. Since it didn't come out, I said, "The hell with it. I'm not going to play it again." I didn't play Sunday, but then the number came out. That made me decide that I should start playing numbers soon.

Did you? Shortly after, I was smoking a cigarette, and between the ash and the paper I saw the numbers two, one, seven. That day, I played a dollar on those numbers and won six hundred dollars.

What did you discover about how people can win? I began researching biorhythms. I saw that when the astrologic cycle was harmonious to my sign and the biorhythms right, I had a better chance of winning, too. In the 1980s, after about two years of playing numbers and winning consistently, I discovered that most of the time when I won it was on my lucky number days.

Did this realization help you formulate your system? Yeah, I saw that people tend to be lucky certain times of the year and certain days of the month, according to their birthday, biorhythms, and astrology combined. Each individual has at least three lucky numbers. Some have four.

Should people write these down? Once the lucky numbers have been determined, people must chart and mark the days. It makes sense to play only on personally desirable days. Many people play every day.

Do you give people these numbers? Sometimes in person or we consult over the phone. Mostly, though, I share my system with people in my book *How to Win Games of Chance.*

What has happened to some of the people who followed your advice? One fellow played with a group, and they picked the numbers. But on the day of the drawing, November 21, he had a feeling to play again, using my system. He said to himself, "I shouldn't play because I've already done it today." But he couldn't get rid of the feeling, and November 21 was one of his lucky days according to my chart.

What did he do? He got to the lottery store just before they closed, and he played his lucky numbers—three, eight, and nine—in different combinations. That night he won the lottery, and the jackpot was three million dollars. He shared it with two other winners. He went on TV afterward and said he used my system.

Give us another case history of someone who used your system. Another man who had just gotten out of the service combined the information in my book with another system and won five million–plus dollars. He also publicly stated that he used my system.

Do you do any psychic consultation for anything other than lottery numbers? I do Kirlian photography through the fingertips. And I read the auras from the photos. Sometimes I see a cartoon character, too; for example, if I see Pinocchio, I know someone is lying.

Can you give an example of what you saw through Kirlian photography? Once I was reading a photo for a woman, and I saw a large car and a small car. The big car was disappearing. When I told her about it, she said she was in the process of a divorce. Her husband was keeping the big car, and she was keeping the small one.

What did you do before you became a lottery psychic? I have left my old field. I am a self-taught artist, and I've won many prizes for my work. I used to have an art gallery and picture framing shop.

Dale W. Emme

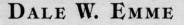

CENTER OF INNER LIGHT
POST OFFICE BOX 644
WESTMINSTER, COLORADO 80030
(303) 427-2707
E-MAIL: Demme644@aol.com

*He's called a "car psychic" because he
sometimes includes people's cars as
part of a psychic session.*

Is the type of car a person owns significant psychically? Yes. I found that whether people had new cars or used ones, I could often relate the condition and problems of their cars with their own personalities, problems, lives, and future.

What about their car is important? I can tell a lot about people based on the model, style, year, and color.

Why would you tell someone something about themselves through their car rather than di-

rectly? For example, if I simply tell someone that they're the type of person who takes too many risks, they might say, "Oh no, I'm very cautious." But using my psychic abilities, I can tell if these people have a red car, seldom drive in the right-hand lane, and drive over the speed limit or too close to the next car. When I tell people all this about themselves, they're more likely to accept my telling them that they're in so much of a hurry to get where they need to go that they're not being careful enough.

Are people more receptive to this than to your just saying what you see about them? For some people, working in metaphysics is too serious an endeavor. It's much easier for many people—especially men—to understand themselves by thinking about their vehicles. And sometimes, just sitting back and enjoying yourself is a way to confront your current situation or problems.

Men especially have trouble looking at where they need to go and at what changes they need to make in their lives. But they are usually very willing to look at what the situation is with their vehicle. If they can relate that back to themselves, then change is fun rather than something serious or frightening.

Are there certain types of situations in which you're more likely to bring up someone's car? Sometimes if an assessment is not entirely positive, it helps to discuss the person's car. For example, some people who are quite withdrawn still fancy themselves as the life of the party. So I can tell that these people drive medium brown or green cars, and I explain their personality to them by discussing their nonflamboyant choice of car color.

Can you also use car color in a positive way? Say they have a white car. White is the color of spirituality and growth. If I point that out, the owner of the white car might be more receptive to a suggestion that he look inside himself to where he's headed in life from a personal and spiritual point of view.

Any other examples? Perhaps a person isn't assertive enough. I may instinctively know then that they drive a black car. When I tell them this, I also tell them they may be trying too hard not to be noticed.

***How can knowing about their car help them in
their life?*** If someone's car has a brake problem and they
haven't rushed to fix it, they may be taking unnecessary
risks or having trouble stopping in life. Showing them this
through their car can be helpful.

***Can you give an example of someone this ap-
proach has helped?*** Someone who had problems with
the starter in his car always had trouble getting to places on
time, getting up in the morning, and getting a job. After I
pointed out that his starter problems were reflected in his
life, he finally straightened up and got a good steady job.
Since then, he also hasn't had any more car starter problems.

Do you use any other tools? Numerology, tarot,
dream interpretation, and past-life regression through hyp-
nosis.

What's your psychic background? My wife and I
both are Cherokee, and my wife, her mother, and her grandmother are all psychics. I didn't really get involved in this
until I met my wife in 1968.

LEAH LUSHER

5941 NORTHEAST 22ND TERRACE
IMPERIAL POINT
FORT LAUDERDALE, FLORIDA 33308
(305) 771-6726
FAX: (305) 771-0237

She won the National Enquirer's *readers' predictions contest twice.*

What happens when you start predicting something? I start to feel a weight on the back of my head, and I know there's going to be some kind of vision. I close my eyes and see a cloud all around me, and then it opens up like a TV screen being turned on. Sometimes I see what's going to happen, and other times I have to interpret it.

How did you get this power? I don't call this a power. I don't know why it happens. Usually I have the cloud, but sometimes an insight will come in a flash.

Can you predict events in your own life? The saddest prediction I made concerned my husband, Tom, a decorated army photographer and a special reporter for the Pentagon. We always had ESP rapport and would tease each other to "stop reading my mind." After all, we wanted our privacy.

On May 13, 1971, he was on a photographic mission in Vietnam. I was at home and had the usual weight on the back of my head, which meant I was going to have a psychic experience. As the fog cleared from my eyes, I saw myself in Vietnam surrounded by our dead boys. Then they lifted a body, and I saw it was Tom. I started screaming and crying.

Did you realize what that meant? I was out of my mind, because from that moment on, I knew he would die. One week later I found out that he had just died.

Describe some of your accurate world predictions? I won the *National Enquirer* psychic prediction contest twice—the only times I entered—against more than two thousand psychics from all over the world.

In 1986, I won fifteen hundred dollars when I got four out of five predictions right. I predicted in 1985 that Soviet leader Leonid Brezhnev, Henry Fonda, and Ingrid Bergman would all die the following year and that Israel would invade Lebanon.

What happened the second time you entered? In 1991, I won again, this time two thousand dollars, after predicting five out of five events correctly: that the following year Sammy Davis, Jr., and Mary Martin would die; that British Prime Minister Margaret Thatcher would be defeated; that civil war would erupt in South Africa; and that Donald Trump would lose a lot of money. Now I do their annual predictions.

Can you see people's auras? Yes, ever since I was a little girl in Italy. It's three or four inches all around the person. If they're aggressive and authoritative, a red aura is emitted. When they're very sick, their aura becomes gray.

Is there anything you don't like about seeing auras? I can see if a person is doomed to die soon because then the aura tends to shrink. Sometimes when I'm watching a person on television, I see this grayish aura. And I say, "Uh-oh, this person is going to die."

Describe a few accurate predictions you've made—not for the world but for your own clients. One woman came to consult me about her marriage, which was in trouble. She said she was fed up with her husband and didn't want him anymore. I had a flash and told her, "Don't worry; your husband doesn't want you anymore either. He has another woman." She seemed insulted and left. But she called back later and said her husband told her he was in love with another woman and wanted a divorce. Then she wanted to know if I could help her get her husband back!

Another case? A young woman in her thirties came to me and said she had decided to divorce her husband because she couldn't stand his mom. I saw the aura around her mother-in-law's face shrink, and my prediction just popped out of my mouth. "Don't divorce him because she's going to drop dead."

Were you right? Two months later the woman called me. "Do you know where I am?" she asked me. "I'm calling you from the funeral home. She dropped dead just like you said."

You're also known for your tea leaf readings. Describe your method. I've been reading tea leaves for twenty years. I drink my tea until it barely covers the leaves. Then I pick the cup up by the handle with my weaker hand. Left-handed people should use their right hand and right-handed their left, because the weaker side is the psychic one.

I swirl the cup seven times and then put it down and look at the bottom, concentrating on the patterns formed by the tea leaves. It's like looking for shapes in clouds. Different ones mean different things. For example, if I see a banana, it means the person will have good luck; a circle means the person will fall in love or have success.

SHAWN ROBBINS

NEW YORK, NEW YORK
(212) 642-6554

She's one of the most famous future forecasters in the country.

Do you think your talents are genetic, perhaps embedded in your DNA somewhere? My mother was born with a veil over her face, the sign of a special gift, usually clairvoyance. In fact, she was a professional psychic, specializing in palm reading. My father was also a natural-born psychic who often saw ghosts wandering through the forests.

What was your first job as a psychic? I decided not to finish high school and, instead, joined an all-woman's band to play pop and cocktail music. After more concerts than I can count and a lot of informal predictions that I made to those around me, I received a telephone call. The caller gave me a pseudonym, mentioned who recommended me, and suggested I meet him. When we met, he identified himself as the vice president of a major U.S. corporation, and he offered me a position as the company's first corporate psychic.

What would your job be? To predict how the general public would respond to new products and new advertising campaigns, beginning with projecting sales figures for a roll-on deodorant several months in advance.

How did you work out? About two months after I joined the firm, I woke up feeling sick and queasy. I warned the company president not to get on the private flight he was scheduled to take that day. He canceled the flight, hired a limousine, and flew on a regularly scheduled flight.

Was there a problem with the plane? I don't know if it would have crashed, but two days after my prediction of problems, it was learned that mechanics had discovered improper installation of the replacement pump on the corporate jet. At the end of that month I received a 50 percent merit raise.

Name some of the many events you predicted. For some reason, I seem to be uniquely attuned to air disasters. My first important prediction, in 1974, described what was at the time the worst air tragedy in aviation history. I said hundreds would be killed en route to London because of a terrorist bomb smuggled on board. I spoke to the FBI, and twelve days after my discussion, a Turkish Airlines DC-10 traveling from Paris to London crashed in the French countryside. A terrorist bomb had caused the crash and 346 people were killed.

Didn't you also get in the news because of your predictions on the Patty Hearst case? Yes. After she was kidnapped, when the whole world was looking for her, an image of her suddenly came to my mind during an interview on Washington TV. I saw her being apprehended by the police. I also got an image of the date of her capture, which seemed to be about September 18 or 19, 1975, and I saw she'd go to jail for a short time and be placed on probation for three years. Her sentence was my exact prediction. My reputation strengthened.

What else have you predicted in the press? I predicted the stock market crash of 1987, known as Black Monday, six months before it happened. The disaster of the space shuttle *Challenger.* The AIDS crisis. The assassination attempt on the life of Pope John Paul. War in Lebanon and the involvement of both the United States and Russia four years before it happened. The Canary Islands crash of two 747s, the biggest air crash in history. I said a member of the IRA would bomb the House of Parliament, and the episode occurred just as I had predicted. I predicted the hostage crisis in Iran and the bombing of the U.S. embassy. While the shah was still in power, I predicted both his overthrow and the emergence of Khomeini as Iran's revolutionary leader.

Can you predict events that aren't major disasters? One day an old high-school friend came to see me. Her father, a man I had known as a child, had been missing for several weeks. As she spoke, I could see her murdered father's body lying in the back seat of a large green car somewhere in midtown New York.

A few weeks later, while investigating an illegally parked truck in a private midtown garage, the police happened to look in the back of a car and discover the green car I had described. In the back seat was my friend's father's body.

When you're working with individuals, do you have a particular way of going about it? Before making any predictions, I try to talk with my client as much as possible. At times, I have an instant vision concerning a person the minute he or she walks in the door. But usually it helps to get to know clients a bit, to learn what is troubling them and what has motivated them to come to me. Generally, I give clients as much information as I can about the near future—up to one year from the time of our session.

Do you do predictions pertaining to gambling? Yes. The first time, a household employee of my mother's came to see me wearing simple, old clothing. She did not ask any questions about her personal life. Instead, she wondered if our meeting had brought any numbers into my mind. I told the number to the client, and she quickly left my apartment.

A few days later, she reappeared, this time wearing a new

dress and a new coat. She again asked for a number. When she arrived for her third visit, she was wearing a fur coat, new shoes, and a fancy dress. Within a few days, she phoned for another appointment and described the new Cadillac she would be driving. I guess my numbers worked.

What do you like best about being able to forecast the future? In small ways, I have been able to help hundreds of friends and strangers foresee and cope with crises and dangers about to erupt in their lives. On the other hand, it hurts me that all too often I have been powerless to prevent major tragedies that in my heart I have known were destined to occur.

What do you predict for the future? In my book, *Prophecies for the End of Time,* which I wrote with Ed Susman, I foresee the following in the year 2000: the end of organ rejections; the admission of Puerto Rico as a fifty-first state; that AIDS will go out of control on the African continent; Cuba will become part of the United States; there will be an interplanetary cataclysm; a war between China, India, and Pakistan; Kervorkian camps—named after the suicide doctor—where people will go to die; and on January 28, 2023, a nuclear power plant disaster will occur in Florida, resulting in the destruction of the coastline and killing forty-eight thousand people.

GEORGE ROMAN

270 NORTH CANON DRIVE, SUITE 1374
BEVERLY HILLS, CALIFORNIA 90210
(310) 289-5129
FAX: (310) 289-1943
E-MAIL: loveguru@netcom.com

Harry Langdon

This love psychic can be found in
Beverly Hills, or on the Internet.

What was your first memory of being psychic?
When I was around nine, I'd often say things off the top of
my head that came true. The first dramatic example I remember involved a woman who had been dating my uncle
for many years. He wasn't popping the question. She was
thinking about splitting, leaving him.

One day I blurted out, "He's going to marry you very
soon. Hang in there! Wait. It will come." The next thing you
know, he gave her the ring and eloped to Vegas with her.

What kind of tools do you use in your work?
Currently I use Vedic (Eastern) astrology from India in doing my readings. It predicts a person's life and destiny as opposed to (Western) astrology, which mainly deals with personality descriptions. But I am not dependent on it.

Do you use anything else? I also read Chinese mahjongg cards. Each card has many different meanings, perhaps as many as five or six interpretations. It's up to the psychic to use his or her powers to tap into what these things are saying precisely.

Using these tools, what do you do for people who come to you? Not only with these tools but also with my own psychic ability, I try to educate people on how to increase their chances of meeting others who share similar goals in life and how to avoid relationships that don't go anywhere. I can clarify what prevents people from having success in their love life.

Who are your clients, and how do you work with them? I have become known as the Beverly Hills Love Psychic. Most people who come to me are interested in their romantic lives. They want to make the right decisions. Is the new man in her life a good match? Is he going to marry her? Should she end a relationship?

How do you tie in Vedic astrology and your psychic abilities? There are planetary periods—called *dasha* periods—that last several years. Birth date, birth time, and birth place are needed, and I can map out a chart that enables me to predict what, when, and where things will happen to an individual.

Incidentally, not every *dasha* is positive. And not everyone goes through every one of the nine *dashas* for each of the planets.

Does all this apply to you as well? Yes. In 1992, I entered into a Venus *dasha* period, which is to last for twenty years. It focuses on romance, sexuality, love, relationships, and the fine arts. So I specialize in love not only because my clients come to me about it but because it fits my own planetary period.

Are most people who come to you women? No, men are also involved in romance, and some men come to me for business and career prospects as well. And not all the people who come to me are private clients. I teach a lot of relationship seminars.

Give an example of a romance you accurately predicted. I had a booth at a Whole Life Expo a couple of years ago. A woman sat down, and I read her cards. I told her that it looked like she was going into a period where her dating life was about to pick up and she was going to get married. "That would surprise me," she replied, "I'm a single mother. I've been living with my son in Arizona, and there's no social activity there. So your reading won't come true."

Did it come true? She stood up to leave, and the man who was running the UFO booth next to mine asked her out for a drink! She and I were shocked. It almost seemed to her like a setup, but it wasn't.

So that was the beginning of the dating experiences I had predicted. Then, a year later, I was doing another expo, and she arrived with another man who was now her husband. She had met him in Arizona, and they had fallen in love and gotten married.

How can people tap into their own psychic gifts? I think the very first instinct or thought is often the psychic one. That's my message to others: Trust your first thoughts.

We're taught from childhood and during our teen years not to trust our initial instincts. We're taught the scientific method in school—that you must be able to prove and validate something, and then it's an accepted fact. With psychic ability, you can't do that. The only proof is when it happens in your life.

If people learn to rely on their first impressions, although they won't always be 100 percent correct, over time they will find they are pretty accurate.

How do you feel about psychic powers? I view them in the same way I view going to the gym. If you go regularly, you'll build up the muscular structure you already have. With psychic ability, the more you trust your thoughts, the more you'll firm and tone your psychic ability.

LAURA STEELE

220 CENTRAL PARK SOUTH, APT. 3D
NEW YORK, NEW YORK 10019
(212) 645-3722
FAX: (212) 956-0727

Alberta Caputo—Lex Labs

*A former child evangelist, she
specializes in location counseling—
either finding lost objects or helping
people who want to relocate.*

***Do you locate objects for people or for compa-
nies?*** Both. People call me who are missing papers, jewelry,
silverware, even a pet snake once. Someone wanted me to
come to their place and look for that snake but I wouldn't—
I was afraid I would find it! Actually I *did* find it for them—
but by phone.

Relate a story of a company that hired you. Made-
moiselle magazine's art department misplaced the lingerie
photos for their upcoming issue. After ten days of looking,
they frantically called me and said they thought the negatives

might have gotten lost in the Paris office since they definitely weren't in New York.

I got strong vibrations on the phone that they *were* in New York, though, and that they were near something royal blue and under something clear. They found them fifteen minutes after our phone call by looking in a clear Lucite box, near a royal blue plastic slide box, in an envelope with royal blue lettering.

Is it easier to find items in person than by phone? I can work just as well either way. I feel the vibrations or energy flow whether I'm physically with the person or on the telephone.

What is your voice vibration reading? As people talk, I get a vision of the room or area that's as clear as the one I get in person. Not only can I see the lost object but I can feel it vibrating all over the place.

How do you help people who are moving to a new location? People call me from all over the world to ask about the prior feelings and spirits of the place they're moving to. Is it a place of brightness and sunshine or are there dark spirits remaining from the previous owners? They also want to be sure that their spiritual guides will travel to the next place with them, and I tell them, "They'll find you."

They want to know if their soul will feel good in the new place because each person feels good when his or her soul is correctly placed.

What is your background? I was the youngest of ten children and became a child evangelist with a Pentecostal church. We traveled with a group all over the South. At thirteen, I was already psychic, and I was popular because I could shout out names and incidents. Others thought it came from God, but it was really my clairvoyant vision that told me these things.

What did you do before you became a psychic? After I left the ministry, I went into real estate. In my early thirties, I went public as a psychic but continued my real estate work because my psychic abilities enabled me to match people with homes that were right for them.

Does your real estate work help you with your geographical counseling? My location counseling ability and my geographical advising skills are helped by the real estate knowledge I have of homes and areas and people's spirits and what blends best.

Can you read everyone? It doesn't matter what the question is or who the person is who is asking it, whether they're sympathetic or skeptical, I can read everyone—but myself. My psychic abilities rarely help me in my own life; except once in a while when I have a little psychic energy attack. For example, when I board a plane, I may tell the flight attendant, "We're going to be delayed."

What is your schedule? In the mornings, I take European calls. Then I take Visa/Mastercard Voice Vibration readings from strangers all over the country, often looking for something or about to move to some place. But I also advise people on everything from romance to careers. *Vogue* wrote that what Dr. Ruth does for the flesh, I do for the spirit.

In the evenings I may do parties, restaurant appearances, and charity benefits. I work until three or four each morning. When I'm not working, I like fishing and cooking.

Do you prefer to do media work on radio or TV? I do both, but I prefer TV, because then people can see that I look normal. Otherwise, some people expect black hats and hanging garlic from a psychic.

ALAN VAUGHAN

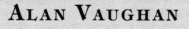

LOS ANGELES, CALIFORNIA
(213) 255-8256
FAX: (213) 257-4242
E-MAIL: AlanPsy@aol.com

Alan Ayazi

Once listed in The Guinness Book of World Records *as the world's most successful predictor, he has many unusual specialties like psychic archaeology and psychic dreaming.*

You were once a skeptic. What made you change? I was originally a science textbook editor and a skeptical researcher of paranormal claims for newspapers and magazines. But I began researching prophecies on my own and found that some of them came true.

How strongly did you go in the other direction? I became the editor of *Psychic* magazine! I remained skeptical about the people who advertised as fortune-tellers; in fact, they were totally worthless. But the ones who worked as mediums at organizations, like psychic research groups and institutions, and reputable psychics who work out of homes and offices—not storefronts—were often very talented.

How did you know? I interviewed dozens of psychics for a research project for the magazine. And there was no doubt that a number of them were able to foresee accurately events in the future, including my future.

What happened during your first psychic experience? In November 1965, at twenty-eight, I was playing with a Ouija board and gave my colleague the exact dates for the beginning and end of the worst blizzard in New York in eighty years. It struck a few months later, as I predicted.

A few weeks after this, I was possessed for twenty-four hours by a spirit named Nada from Nantucket, who came through the Ouija board. After that twenty-four-hour period, my higher self told me I was a spirit, and I felt this tremendous energy rising up that pushed Nada out of my head and instantly I became psychic.

How did you feel? I never felt so good before. I could sense other dimensions of reality. From that moment on, I could sense the future and what was in people's minds. I then burned the Ouija board because I thought it was so dangerous.

What type of work have you done in psychic archaeology? In 1987, I became involved in locating a Spanish treasure ship in the waters off the Bahamas. I predicted it would take seven years to find it. In 1994, the ship was located, with initial finds of emeralds and gold coins. Salvage begins soon.

Any other cases? Many, but also in 1987, while I was on a research vessel, I described a 150-year-old ship lying buried on the ocean floor off the Bahamas. They dropped a buoy in the water and it was only thirty-five feet away from where I said it would be.

Are you doing some work in this area now? I am currently working with a new group to locate history's most fabulous sunken treasure ship. It carried priceless jeweled gifts sent by the king of Siam to the French king Louis XIV that have been lost for three centuries. I believe I've located it in the Indian Ocean, and we're going back to do a survey with a salvage ship.

What about psychic dreaming? Psychic dreams are when you dream about people and actions that are distant or in the future. I did a lot of work on this, and I wrote a book on it called *Incredible Coincidence*.

How do you do it? When I'm awake, I try to see a picture in response to a target question. These pictures are like movies or videos. But I can also do this while I'm sleeping. Twenty-eight percent of my recorded dreams have predicted events in my future.

Has it had practical application for you? I ended up in Los Angeles in 1980 because one of my dreams gave me the area code 213.

What other type of work have you done? In readings, writings, lectures, and seminars, I've taught intuitive techniques to twenty thousand people over twenty-five years and have developed computer software to help people learn it.

How are you spending most of your professional time now? Most of my work now is with private clients who want the answers to question like where to find a job, where to find a house, and where to find a mate. In addition, I work with individuals and organizations doing crime work, specializing in murder and missing persons' cases. But I will not work on cases in which organized crime is involved. I don't want them coming after me!

How can people develop their predictive ability? Think of an event in the future, like something that happens every year. Let yourself go forward in time and *look* at it rather than describe it. Give yourself target questions, and then try to see a picture of the response, since pictures are better than words.

What is your greatest accomplishment? The Central Premonitions Registry in New York was a research project involving premonitions and predictions of the future.

They recorded predictions from thirty-five hundred people in twenty-eight countries over a twenty-year period, from 1968 until 1988.

What were some of your fulfilled predictions? Those recorded with them included the Watergate scandal, Nixon's resignation, the launching time of the first space shuttle, and the *Apollo 13* and *Challenger* disasters. For these and others, I ended up in *The Guinness Book of World Records* as "the world's most successful predictor" in the psychic category.

Voxx

8489 WEST 3RD STREET, SUITE 1035
LOS ANGELES, CALIFORNIA 90048
(213) 882-4162
(213) 782-0222
FAX: (213) 655-6207

Claire Shubert Taylor

A multimedia artist and psychic, this love psychic serves Hollywood's "brat pack" and younger community.

Who is your clientele? In the seven years that I've been in full-time practice, I have developed a database of fifteen thousand clients. I have read for many of the young celebrities in L.A., including Drew Barrymore, River Phoenix, members of the Zappa family, and Carnie Wilson, among others.

Why did you become a love psychic? I like to help people with love problems.

Give an example of your success here. One time I was reading for a woman who hadn't had a date in two years. I told her that she'd meet her husband in less than three months, and I predicted she'd be engaged by the end of the year. I told her what to change in her life to make romance happen.

Did you foresee her future husband? I even described her future husband: a thirty-eight-year-old Capricorn with dark hair and mustache who worked as a police officer. He had a three-year-old daughter, who was a Pisces; he was just out of a divorce and had a nasty ex-wife. He was Caucasian, and she was black. I told my client they'd meet through the mail, and *everything* happened as I said.

Do you ever predict that love would go awry? Sometimes I predict that people will *not* marry. A girl came to see me who was already engaged and planning to marry. She had the date set, her dress bought. I said, "Sorry, no marriage to this guy. He will upset you before the wedding."

Then her future husband could not accept what the priest required for a lifelong commitment, and consequently, the priest refused to sanction the marriage so the young man broke it off.

What is your main interest outside of the spiritual world? Music is my field. I sing, write music, and play many instruments. I played in my college symphony and toured England with a band after college, and I have some musical albums out.

How do you keep the two pursuits in your life separate? I can't always do it. For example, once, when I was playing the conga drums in a recording studio—and drums are not my strong suit—I began playing pieces that would be difficult for a good drummer. I believe an entity took over my body and played the drums for two hours. That kept my hands from wearing out. I wrote everything that happened that night in my journal and then floated outside my body. That was also my first astral experience.

What entity played the drums for you? I was receiving instructions clairaudiently from the Rhythm Master. He's the one who gave me the name Voxx, which means voice, and told me to use my voice for something important.

Do you have psychic roots? I am a natural-born psychic on both sides of my family. On my father's side, I am a descendant of Malcolm III, king of Scotland, plus Aleister Crowley and other famous mystics, philosophers, and occult figures of the last hundred years. My maternal grandmother was a well-known community healer in the Lower East Side of New York in the '20s and '30s.

And your own psychic background? I was born in Ethiopia and raised in Saudi Arabia and the United States. I started studying astrology and reading tarot at seven. When I was ten years old, I started seriously studying the occult. I grew up playing "Guess What I'm Thinking?" with my two sisters. My parents taught me to interpret dreams, omens, and signs. We used to discuss our dreams at the breakfast table. I've been reading cards for others since I was twelve.

What type of psychic experiences did you have when you were young? I always loved to go to stores with my mother and point out who was pregnant and who was ill. I would look at photographs and say, "Look, Mom, this person is sleeping with that one." Sometimes, my mom would kick me in the shins to stop me from commenting on someone or something.

Did your psychic abilities help you in school? It made it very easy for me. I knew the answers. If I was taking a science test, I could just visualize the textbook and go back to the page where I underlined the correct answers to the test. I skipped the twelfth grade in school.

And in work? Just before I became a professional psychic, I typed for some law firms. But I was always reading everyone's thoughts and feelings. I could see who didn't like me—and who would fire me!

RON WARMOTH

POST OFFICE BOX 4037
LOS ANGELES, CALIFORNIA 90078
(213) 389-3483
FAX: (213) 389-6211

*He's been called a human metal
detector because of his success in
locating minerals.*

How do you feel about your gift? I never believed
I had a grand gift. I was just born with certain abilities,
which I never realized were any different from anyone else's.
I've never known any other way to be. To me my work is
common; to someone else it may be rare or interesting.

Why do they call you a human Geiger counter?
Because I have discovered hundreds of millions of dollars'
worth of oil and precious metals, like gold, silver, uranium,
and even a gas well where no gas was ever found before.

What was your greatest success? Locating six oil

strikes that made more than three hundred million dollars for the owners.

Give an example of an oil success. The *Los Angeles Times* wrote that an oil producer gave me a map showing fifteen sites where geologists had already tested for oil. There was no way I could have known the results of the test drillings. I selected six sites and said the others were dry. I was 100 percent accurate. The oilman has since become a client.

How about a success story with metal? Another one of my clients was a part-time miner who spent years digging in Montana for silver. I drew a map of his property, which was perfect, even though I had never been there. I told him he was right on target, almost on top of it. What he found turned out to be more valuable than silver. It was a mixture of gold and platinum.

How do you work? I operate differently than most psychics because I am not a fortune-teller. People don't come to me for predictions as much as for physic insight. I work extensively with the business community, primarily the mining and oil industry. Psychically, I can locate underground springs, gas, and metals.

I use a form of psychic dowsing, which is not as strange as some people think. Dickens and Einstein were said to have dabbled in dowsing.

Do you take a percentage? None, and I don't mine myself because I wouldn't have the vaguest idea how to get ore out of a mine.

Can you outline step by step how you work? I start by examining maps the client brings to me. If I receive no impression, I'll return them to the client. But if I see shadows, I pinpoint them with a pencil. It's like *déjà vu*, as if I saw the map yesterday, marked by someone else to tell me where the minerals are. These messages are like thought waves. I believe it's a breakoff from my subconscious mind.

Can you pick up on what people are thinking? I don't try to pick up on private affairs. But business affairs fascinate me. I'm not interested in people's love relationships—anyone coming to me for information on marriage would be extremely disappointed.

How accurate are you? I don't make grand claims. I'm not a wizard. I do my best, but I'm not always accurate. As I told *Newsweek,* I tell people to take my advice like that of an attorney or a doctor: Get other opinions from geologists and other mining experts. I could be wrong. But most of the time I'm not.

How about the stock market? Have you been able to mine any money out of that? I've also been fortunate and accurate in predictions about the stock market, but I don't know if it's from psychic abilities or common sense. I think a lot of psychic predictions are nothing more than educated guesses. Successful businesspeople rely on hunches, which are a form of ESP. Some people just develop their ESP to a higher extent than others.

How close do you become with your clients? I spend long periods of time with them. I get involved with businesses and people in a particularly personal and intense way. I am one person they can talk to without having gossip about their business spread all over town.

My reward comes in seeing the person develop his or her full potential or the full potential of his or her company. I feel this is my function in life.

How did you get started? My mother encouraged my talents. She would make me guess objects inside a box. Or she'd think of a word, number, or shape and test my ability to pick it up. I was almost always right.

Presumably, you didn't grow up wanting to be a human Geiger counter. What did you want to do in life originally? I wanted to be an actor. At twenty-two or twenty-three, right out of college, I moved to New York to perform in summer stock. There I received an offer to work in L.A., where I met a retired psychic living in my apartment complex who was doing a mentalist act.

I began exploring the possibilities of this kind of work and discovered that I had natural abilities. I initiated my psychic career in a small coffeehouse. Using strong telepathy, I picked up specific names, places, dates. Then an interview with me for *Fate* magazine established my credibility.

Have you done any other kind of psychic work?
I attract business clientele, but I've done it all: public reader, white-collar crime, political work for both parties, police work.

Give an example of your crime work. I was involved in helping the police on a kidnap–sexual molestation case of a nine-year-old girl. There were ten instances in southern California in which this man would lure girls from six to twelve years old into his car to look for his lost dog. The Lost Dog Rapist, as he was called, would then drive the girls to another location and sexually assault them.

I saw that the rapist had a name like James or Jim; his last name started with the letter *F* and sounded like Flory; he was thirty-nine or older, and a Caucasian with dirty brown hair.

When the Lost Dog Rapist was finally found, it turned out his alias was James Ferri. He was forty-two years old and Caucasian.

GEORGE R. WITHERS

31 EGRET CIRCLE
DENVER, PENNSYLVANIA 17517
(717) 336–2998
E-MAIL: http://www.syspac.com/~thorne/page1.htm

He reads candles through crystal balls.

Describe your candle readings. I keep the room dark
except for a lighted candle, which is about three inches in
diameter and nine inches long. I keep this candle between
me and my client so he or she can focus completely on it.
When clients come in, I begin each session with the Lord's
Prayer to let the highest and best come in. Then I have them
gaze at the flickering flame for a while to relax them, because
some people come in very tense—they've had a fight with
their mate or they've lost their job—and you've got to relax
them to read them. So I burn the white candle for a while,
and that almost always calms them down.

What next? Then I hold a crystal ball above the candle,
which magnifies the flame. Some people think I'm reading
the crystal ball, but I'm really using it to read the candle.

I look into the hole in the bottom of the flat part of the crystal ball, and I can read all sorts of things in this white energy—the Christ energy.

What can you visualize? I can see scenes, initials, possible trips the person may take, health, family, job, career, investments, travel, marriage, education, and love life. I may see the person sitting in a conference or in a lawyer's office. Or I may see them on a yacht. Sometimes I see death in someone's future, but those are things I don't want to predict. Being a psychic is a great responsibility.

Do you do anything after the candle reading? The reading is followed by a crystal ball confirmation and detailing of the advice and revelations. Finally comes a tarot reading.

Describe an interesting case of something you've seen in a candle. One woman came to me, and I saw in the candle that there was a woman's hand with a square onyx ring on it. The hand was reaching stealthily into a cash register and taking money out. I said to her, "Your business seems to be good, but it's losing money." And when I described the ring I saw, she said, "That's my cashier. She's been with me for years. She wouldn't possibly steal."

Did she do anything about what you saw? Although she was disbelieving, she began watching her cashier more carefully. She saw that some of her receipts were misnumbered or missing. Then she realized that when the cashier would open up the drawer to give someone, say five dollars in change, she might take the twenty the customer gave her and put that in her pocket!

What type of people come to you? I'm like the court of last resort for some of them. They've already been to doctors and lawyers. I think of myself as a resource person; in addition to giving them a candle reading, I may tell them where they can find the help they need.

You live pretty far away from the mainstream. Where do your clients come from? People come from all over the country. Plus I have a large clientele right here in Pennsylvania, which amazes me because I live in the heart of Amish country in ultraconservative Lancaster County.

Do you also give lectures or speeches? Some psychics can razzle-dazzle audiences, but I'm better at one-to-one.

MORE SUPERSPECIALISTS

MARY T. BROWNE

92 HORATIO STREET
NEW YORK, NEW YORK 10014
(212) 242-6080

Specialty: Spirit communication

JOAN CARRA

TRS, INC., PROFESSIONAL SUITE
44 EAST 32ND STREET
NEW YORK, NEW YORK 10016
(212) 685-2848
E-MAIL: JORDANIA12@aol.com

Specialty: Extraterrestrial communication

BARBARA CONNOR

2020 WEST ALAMEDIA, APT. 2K
ANAHEIM, CALIFORNIA 92801
(714) 635-8919

Specialty: Ghost hunter, haunted house exploration

JIM AND PAT FREGIA

POST OFFICE BOX 52
PAGOSA SPRINGS, COLORADO 81147
(970) 731-2797
E-MAIL: Dreamer521@aol.com

Specialty: Teaching dream interpretation

MARIE GRACIETTE

NORTH HOLLYWOOD, CALIFORNIA
(818) 506-6506

Specialty: Readings in Spanish and Portuguese

MERRYN JOSE-SCHLOSSBERG

C/O CASTLE HILL PRODUCTIONS
1414 AVENUE OF THE AMERICAS
NEW YORK, NEW YORK 10019

Specialty: Rearranging one's future

PATRICIA MISCHELL

POST OFFICE BOX 1238
CINCINNATI, OHIO 45201
(513) 563-1744
FAX: (513) 563-1671

Specialty: Spirit contact and communication

JOAN RUTH WINDSOR, M.ED.

PERSONAL DEVELOPMENT INSTITUTE
POST OFFICE BOX 1056
WILLIAMSBURG, VIRGINIA 23187
(804) 229-4873

Specialty: Dream analysis

CHAPTER
6

Channelers and
Automatic Writers

JOHN HARRICHARAN, M.B.A.

1401 JOHNSON FERRY ROAD, SUITE 328-M7
MARIETTA, GEORGIA 30062
(770) 977-9035
FAX: (770) 971-0412
E-MAIL: jhh711@aol.com

Once a Fortune 500 executive who lost everything, he's written two inspirational best-sellers by automatic writing.

How do you feel about New Age people? When I speak to a New Age group, I tell them, "Half of you are nuts and half of you are sane, and I can't tell the difference.

What is your background? I was born to East Indian parents in Guyana and grew up on the northern coast of South America. Later, I graduated summa cum laude in chemistry and mathematics and got an M.B.A. I had a successful international business that made me a millionaire before I was forty. Before that, I also worked for several

Fortune 500 corporations. Meanwhile, I had a fairy-tale marriage to the princess of my dreams.

What did you learn when your life collapsed around you? My wife died in her thirties after fighting cancer for three years, leaving me with two children. Around the same time, I lost my business and all my earthly possessions. Even my car was repossessed, and I had to start again from ground zero.

In time, I realized that while I didn't understand everything that was going on or why, there *was* a reason for it. It was just that I didn't have all the data, and I wasn't seeing all the parts.

It was like seeing a rug being woven from the back, before you can see the pattern. And I came to realize that one day I would understand the deeper meaning—and that there would be one. As Einstein said, "God doesn't play dice with the universe." There is an order to it all.

I recognized that I would have to *grow* through life, not just *go* through it. And to help me do that, I would have to develop a deeper personal relationship with God.

How did you start to pull your life together? I decided that building a life was more important than building a fortune. I wanted to write, but I didn't just think about it. I had to take the necessary steps. It's like the joke about the man who goes to church every day and keeps praying, "Oh, God, let me win the lottery!" And one day from the back of the room comes this booming voice saying, "Give me a break! Buy a ticket!"

My first book, *When You Can Walk on Water, Take the Boat,* came through me via automatic writing. My second book was about my wife and family, and it was written the same way.

Describe the process of automatically writing a book. Recently, I sat down, picked up my pen, and the words "Journey in the Fields of Forever" came out. And I said, "Wonderful, flowing, what does this mean?" And that weekend I wrote the entire final draft of my third book.

Throughout my writing, I felt the presence of my wife right there. When I'm doing automatic writing, I always feel the essence of close ones near me. The air changes and the temperature drops a few degrees. At times there's a stillness, and sometimes I hear music.

How can you be sure that you didn't write your books? I couldn't have thought up some of those things I wrote. I've read them and said, "Wow, that's good." And maybe I did write them. If words come from deep within you or way outside you, it's all one, so it doesn't matter. How do I know where one entity starts and the other begins? I claim I wrote them, my name is on them, and I'm getting the royalties.

Do you think ESP has practical applications? There's no doubt that it saves lives. Several years ago, I was working as a production manager and deciding who was going to work on which shift. I pulled out the paper and I started saying to the people around me, "You, James, will work on tomorrow's shift." But when I went to write that in, I couldn't write it. And a strange feeling came over me that said, "Cancel the shift tomorrow."

The following day, around three, I got a call saying, "Thank goodness you didn't have anyone working here. There was a horrible explosion and someone would have been killed. The fire trucks are here now."

What happens when we die? No one actually dies. If we love someone and they love us, we are always in touch. I still feel my wife's presence, and I get data from her that helps me. I also get little signs from my son of things she has said to him since she died, things that could only come from her.

Death is just beyond that door and the curtain is very thin, and every once in a while the curtain parts and we get a glimpse of what's on the other side. Once we get there, if we were terrible here, we don't instantly get transformed into angels. We have to work for it. We have to learn. It's a process of evolution in the other life.

KURT LELAND

POST OFFICE BOX 911
JAMAICA PLAIN, MASSACHUSETTS 02130
(617) 524-2669

Brian Galford

He's a former musician and now a channeler through "Charles," and his clientele includes artists and commodities brokers.

What was it like when you first started channeling? An entity by the name of Charles came to me during a trance, and he has been with me ever since as the guide who does the readings for people. It really was startling the first time I spoke in trance to have the feeling that there was some other consciousness present in my body.

There was a period some years ago when Charles occasionally would come through and want to say something to someone I was having dinner with. That was awkward because the waiter might come and start serving the food just at the moment I was saying something really intense with my eyes closed!

Do you still have to go into a trance to talk to him? No, now he's present anytime I need him to whisper in my ear some little piece of guidance about something I'm busy with or to tell me whether what someone is telling me about themselves is true or what it really means.

Do you like channeling for those who passed on? No, I have found that really disturbing. One teenage girl's boyfriend had broken up with her, and she had attempted suicide with sleeping pills to prove she really loved him. She hadn't really wanted to die, but she overdosed. And she didn't believe she was dead. She just kept saying over and over again, "I'm going to wake up. I'm going to wake up."

When we got the date she had died, it was fifteen years before the séance. That kind of thing really does shake me up. You'd like to help spirits like that move beyond where they are, but when they're inside of you, talking through you, and their thoughts are in you, it's a little like being slimed.

Are you conscious while you channel? Yes, although I tend not to remember specifically what I say after an hour or two. But when I come out of a trance, I'm often able to remember the *topics* that were talked about.

I feel that I'm present in the trance as a kind of an audience, listening to what's being said. This helps me a lot because when something is being said that benefits me and my growth, I'll recall that and be able to take it with me out of the trance.

How does Charles help people? My philosophy, or Charles's philosophy, is that if someone is experiencing problems it's probably because the ego is moving in a direction different from one the soul would wish. So what Charles tries to do is to lay out the soul's plan for people.

Explain this. Usually, Charles will get some information from the person, so there is a real clear idea of what the ego's perspective on a thing is, and then he will start demonstrating how that relates to the soul's perspective and what can be done to make changes.

Charles also uses dream analysis, which is important as a means of receiving nightly reports on how one is progressing in realizing the soul's master plan.

What type of clients do you have? I have many commodities brokers, but I don't do predictive work around what the market is going to do.

Why? From the spiritual perspective, whether you come in on the short or long side of a trade doesn't really matter so much. What matters is being clear enough that you can follow the flow of energy that's going through the trading pit at the time the decisions are being made. Then you are able to make money. And because I have a musical background, I also have a lot of musicians and artists as clients.

When did you first become interested in the other realm? I guess you can say that something was going on in that department pretty much all my life. But I didn't have a crisis in my life the way I've read some people have before they become absorbed in psychic pursuits. I was in graduate school studying music, I was bored, and I just wanted to find something else.

What is Charles's philosophy? One of the things Charles says is that happiness is in the opposite direction of what you tell yourself it is. Emotional pain is the result of denied expectations. If you want to live a life of suffering and misery, then pursue what you think will make you happy.

BETTY MUENCH

1202 ALVARADO DRIVE, NORTHEAST
ALBUQUERQUE, NEW MEXICO 87110

Kim Jew Photography Studio

*She channels at the typewriter through
her spirit guides.*

Were you always psychic? No, I ran a piano store and
music center with my husband until we were divorced on
April Fools' Day, 1977. He was a flyer. In fact, he died in a
stunt show in 1978.

How did his plane crash? He was trying to do a triple
loop but had accidentally set the altimeter two hundred feet
short, which crashed the plane into the ground. Three years
prior to his death, while doing readings for myself, I had
gotten about seventeen references to his dying.

When did you discover you were psychic? I used
to think psychic things were silly. I was a logical businessper-
son. Then, while visiting some friends in San Francisco, I

began dabbling with the Ouija board as a game. When we started using the Ouija board, an entity told me, "Go home." I said, "I am going home." Then I asked if I were to go home and get a Ouija board, would I get an answer from the entity. The answer was affirmative.

What was your reaction? I was not thrilled. I didn't think I wanted to get into the unknown.

Did you have any further experiences with the Ouija board? I couldn't resist buying one for myself, and every evening, I would go to the board and typewriter. In the beginning, nothing of interest happened. But about two months later, the board was all over the place.

What was it saying? "WL U KM—WL U KM?" I had not read any books about altered states, meditation, or self-hypnosis. I didn't know what was happening. The planchette kept going back and forth, back and forth like a pendulum. I would lean back, and it would pull toward my middle and stop. Then I heard in my ear, "Write. Write. Write."

What did it say when you started writing? Immediately, I was told in that first message that I would do four things: see and hear the future, travel without leaving home, and do healings. Since then, through readings, I have had clairvoyant visions, clairaudient messages (which is inner telepathic hearing), and astral projections and have helped heal the hurts of others.

Describe a session with a client. I cover three subjects or three compound questions at a time. I type them in the beginning of the reading, and then I have the client ask them one at a time during the session. I type without stopping and without punctuation and then read it back. That is when we discuss it and see if we can learn something.

What questions do most people ask? The true purpose in this lifetime is the number-one question, like Who am I? and What am I doing here on earth? Relationships follow.

Are there any questions you won't answer? Long ago I stopped answering clients who wanted to know, "Will I be rich?" I am not a fortune-teller.

Do you get any help in answering the questions?

I work with a group entity, spirit guides that came individually at first but expanded and are now called Friends in Source.

What is your schedule for readings? I learned early in this work that I cannot schedule people back to back as they do in a doctor's office. I now work mostly by mail with clients all over the world, holding samples of the handwriting to get vibrations of the person. This is psychometry, and I also use it to tap into the energy of a person, using not only handwriting but personal objects like watches. They're good because they absorb a great deal of energy because people wear their watches all the time, not just on special occasions.

What was the most interesting thing to happen to you? I met George Bush in 1978 at a Republican fundraiser. We were at a cocktail party before dinner. I was looking out the window, and a good-looking man asked me, "What are you doing here besides looking beautiful?" He must have thought I was a wealthy Republican fat cat.

We talked about tennis, the weather, books. I told him I thought politicians should stop talking down to people because the population was more enlightened.

Then I mentioned a book called *Inner Tennis,* where you psyche out your opponent. He asked how much I knew about "the psychic thing." I waved my hand, indicating so-so.

It was George Bush, and he turned out to be the speaker for the evening. During the course of his speech, he stated that politicians must stop talking down to their constituents.

The audience applauded wildly.

ROBERT PETRO

SEDONA, ARIZONA
(520) 282-6522

He couldn't read until he was thirty-two, but now this trance channeler can read everything, including the future.

How was your childhood unique? I had a learning disability, and I was considered a problem child by my parents. I ended up in children's shelters—places like Boys Town—and even reform school. That hurt me personally because I knew I was not a bad boy. But I could not read, write, or spell until I was thirty-two. The first book I read was *Old Yeller,* and I cried.

Did you have any psychic experiences in the orphanages and reform schools? Yes, my first major psychic experience occurred when I was eleven. I slept in a dormitory with thirty other boys. One night I fell asleep and saw a brilliant light at the end of the bed. In it was a beautiful woman wearing a garment with a white hood. I could only see her face, hands, and feet. I was terrified. I saw myself fall to her feet. When I opened my eyes, she was gone. I related the incident to the Catholic brother, but he thought I was lying and beat me.

Did you keep quiet about it after that? I went home and told my sister's mother-in-law, a devout Catholic. She explained that the Blessed Mother had appeared to me and that I would become a special person. I accepted her wisdom with disbelief, as life for me was a disaster until then.

When did life start to improve for you? I was married at twenty-three and had three children immediately. I had a wonderful family, but I had business problems because I entered the adult world without tools to achieve.

I took a job as a delivery boy for a flower shop. Then I became a flower designer. One year after that I bought the business.

What happened to change your life around? One day a handsome, refined man came into the shop. I told him something about his life that was correct. He returned one hour later with a book. I had just learned to read that month.

When I read this second book, I realized I had the same talent as the man in the book and that my ability to see things in a trance wasn't the curse that I thought it was. I wanted to be just like the man in the book. The man was Edgar Cayce.

What was your most eerily accurate prediction? I was lecturing in Hartford, Connecticut, before an audience of seven or eight hundred people when someone spouted off, "If you're so psychic, tell us the headlines of tomorrow's paper."

What did you tell them? "Upstairs in this hotel are three men who will rob a bank tomorrow morning." After the robbery occurred the next morning, the FBI interrogated me and even tracked down some participants in my seminar to make sure there was no connection between me and the robbery. But that was the only time I was happy to learn of a bank robbery.

What is your specialty? Finding missing bodies and working on criminal cases. Some I have worked on have been well known, like the case of Peter Reilly—a sixteen-year-old boy accused of killing his mother—which became the basis for a book and movie called *A Death in Canaan*. I worked with the state police and I predicted the outcome of the entire case: I said that he was innocent, that there would be a new trial, and that the charges would be dropped. I was right.

What do you feel during your trances? During my trances, you would never know that I was feeling anything, but I am feeling *everything*. Many of my cases have upset me very much. One time, the killer cut off the arms, legs, and head of the victim. Another time, two students were stabbed thirty-seven times, and their throats were cut.

Has this all ever gotten to you? I worked on the case of an eight-year-old girl who was brutally raped and murdered. I saw her body and gave information on it. That night at home with my three daughters, I had flashbacks of the little girl's rape and murder.

All the crimes I had worked on had become too much for me. I went upstairs, crying. Beneath my talent was a human being who was having a terrible time coping and not showing stress.

I left the house with a gun and checked into a hotel. I put the gun in my mouth. I heard a loud explosion. I woke up with the gun in my hand, believing that a ball of fire had exploded in my face and knocked me out. I don't know what happened, but I realized I was not meant to kill myself.

What are your most satisfying cases? One night while I was sleeping, I heard a girl sobbing. I realized it was one of my students, who was attempting suicide in her car. I got dressed and went out to look for her. I drove the back roads until I found her and stopped her.

What are some other illustrations of your gift? Another man came to me because his wife and son were missing. I went into a trance, and I saw that she was with a male friend. I didn't know what to do. If I told the husband that his wife was sleeping with this man, he would kill her.

What did you tell him? He talked to me on a Monday. All I told him was she would be home by Friday, but I didn't say where she was. When the woman came back to him, she confessed everything.

How did he take it? The man was furious and came back to me. He sent her and his son to her mother in Mexico, and then he hired a killer to get them there. I convinced him not to kill his wife, then went to Mexico and stopped the killers he had hired.

Have you done any international cases? I became like a pet for the Russian embassy. I did so many cases with them. On one occasion, a Russian agent, who was involved in some sort of covert activity, came to see me. He had been shot, and blood was dripping while I was reading for him.

What other interesting things have you done? I helped one of the Vanderbilts communicate with her deceased husband. I've performed exorcisms. In 1989 I moved to Santa Fe, New Mexico, where I was a medicine man with the Navajo Indians.

What do you do now? Two years ago, I relocated to Sedona, Arizona, where I teach metaphysical and Shaman medicine. I am also a psychic practitioner, working with private clients and different agencies. I like teaching the best.

SUSAN LEE SHAW

4440-I SHADOW HILLS CIRCLE
SANTA BARBARA, CALIFORNIA 93105
(805) 683-9018
FAX: (805) 967-7978

Susan Lee Shaw, who has a law degree, channels her information through her spirit guide, Elvis Presley.

What was your relationship with Elvis Presley?
When I was young, I lived in Bel Air and met Elvis through the singers, Jan and Dean. After he became famous, I was his mistress and confidante from 1963 until he passed over in 1977.

Others have said he was very spiritual. Was that true? Oh yes, it was his mission to prove that there is life after death. We both planned for me to be his voice box after his lifetime. Many times he told me that he would keep in contact with me and let me know how life progressed on the other side.

Did he? He started right after he died. I was driving and got a clear vision of him and he said to me, "I'm at home. I'm really at peace."

What is his life like now? I noticed he wasn't wearing his glasses, which he usually did. He told me that he was in perfect health, that there was no need for glasses.

Another time, he told me about his life in heaven, where he hates to be called "the Pelvis." He said there is no entertainment there. He has become the Mother Teresa of dead rock and rollers. He heals the sick and helps struggling composers. He hates all the live sightings of himself, and he plans to return to the mortal plane as his own granddaughter by Lisa Marie.

Did you ever discuss these kinds of things with him when he was here? We knew from the time when he was alive that we had many past lives together, but it was the early '60s, and people didn't talk as openly about these things.

Does Elvis give you advice? A few years ago, Elvis told me to get out of L.A. and move to Santa Barbara, which I did. I can tune him in any time. It's like a radio or TV. When I see something, it's like a lightning bolt, but I can turn it off. Otherwise I'd go crazy.

Do you tell your clients about your relationship with Elvis? I don't like to make a big deal out of Elvis's being my spirit guide when I'm doing my private readings. I say, "This is what I'm getting," not "This is what Elvis says." I also don't tell everyone I meet that I'm psychic because that makes some people nervous that you can read their mind.

Who are your clients? Because I have a law degree, I do a lot of businesspeople, and I'm good at predicting stock market crashes and business cycles. I also have a real estate license, so I do brokers and real estate agents as well.

Did your family play a role in your metaphysical development? My mother and grandmother were psychics, and I now know I was psychic as a child. I felt that I was not only clairvoyant but clairaudient and clairsensuous, that is, I could see, hear, and feel psychically.

Were there any watershed events in your psychic history? I remember telling my mother that my aunt and uncle, who were supposed to move into a new home, would not. A day before they were going to move, my uncle had a heart attack and died, so they didn't move.

Was there anything else that opened your eyes to psychic matters? I became interested in genealogy through my brother and his wife who are Mormons. I started by studying the families of famous people. With my psychic ability, I could trace people back into their past lives. Then I saw I could not only read the past but predict the future for them.

See: Terry and Linda Jamison, page 57.
Ruth Montgomery, page 299.

CHAPTER
7

Psychic Astrologers and Healers

WENDY Z. ASHLEY

POST OFFICE BOX 14
PEAKS ISLAND, MAINE 04108
(207) 766-5108

Copyright Carol Clayton Photography

She is a psychic astrologer who specializes in myths and symbols.

Did your family have anything to do with your spirituality? My mother was psychic. She was tested at the Psychical Research Society in New York in the 30s. Not only did I grow up with a psychic mother but with a psychic aunt and a psychic grandfather.

Did that make the psychic world more attractive to you? No, I knew what psychic stuff was all about, and I didn't think it was very attractive. Odd was more like it. The last thing I wanted was to be a weirdo like my mom.

Why did you choose to use mythic or symbolic astrology instead of more conventional methods for your clients? I found that astrology was too judgmental of people. I wanted to find something that made it truer. I started using symbols and mythology.

Explain mythic or symbolic astrology. We're all taught to look at things rationally and realistically. Anytime we think of things in an irrational way, we're told that we're wrong. We learn that dreams are just dreams and movies are just movies and anything that can't be seen is sort of fanciful and not real.

How did this change your way of looking at a client's situation? When I learned to think imaginally and mythologically, it suddenly opened up what people's lives were about that was not available to me before as a practicing astrologer.

As I worked with symbols, I understood a great deal more than I could have known through rational linear thought. I began to "see" in this way of thinking and accessed information that most of us miss. The rational world discounts or ignores clues that go on all the time.

Give an example. Some people think that dreams are purely psychic events, so if you dream there's a tree in your backyard, it can mean many things.

Symbolic astrology brings up what a backyard is, what a tree is, whether you had a tree in a backyard at some other time in your life, what kind of tree it is, what is the symbolic nature of this tree, what the tree means to your psychology and your spiritual life, and maybe the tree in reference to a myth, since there are many myths that involve trees.

Has thinking like this expanded the way you view a situation? I have learned to reach my mind out in dozens of directions, almost simultaneously, to get this holistic perspective, with each part capable of being broken down into a symbolic meaning.

Is this type of thinking very unusual? This intuitive prerational way of thinking is essentially the kind of thinking that "wise" men, magicians, and gurus are capable of. Westerners think that this is some superhuman quality, but it's not.

Give an example of how you've been able to help a client utilizing this approach. A young man came to see me whose mythology was very much of Dionysus. Like Dionysus, the god of dance in ancient Greece, this man was a dancer, nineteen or twenty years old. He had been totally rejected by his overly moral, righteous family because he was gay and they were mortified. This was troubling him terribly.

Where did symbolic astrology come into this? I saw that this was not just his problem but that the family had dealt with this before and that his father's brother was gay and it was very traumatic for the family. But he said that his father didn't have a brother, although my interpretation of his horoscope indicated that he did.

What did he do about the information you gave him? He went and asked his great-aunt, and from her, he discovered that his father's brother was gay. The brother had gone out to Hollywood to be in the film business, and his grandparents had totally disowned him. My client found this uncle, looked him up, and this was the beginning of a healing in his family.

Where did the psychic elements come into this case? Now, although this was initially mythological and astrological, it was because of the intuitive work that I could assert that, yes, indeed, his father did have a brother! Ultimately, my psychic intuition was what started him on this healing path with his family.

DOUGLAS JOHNSON

951 MICHELTORENA STREET
LOS ANGELES, CALIFORNIA 90026
(213) 663-9067

*This former banker is now a
psychic healer.*

Describe your first significant psychic experience. When I was born, both my mother and I almost died.
She had a critical heart condition, which I inherited. One
day I was playing with a friend, and I heard a voice calling
me from what seemed like the ceiling: "Doug, your mother
will die tonight." I knew it was true even though the doctors
thought she was better. She did die; I was nine, and that was
my first psychic experience.

Incidentally, many doctors confirmed that I was doomed
with the same horrible heart condition as my mother. At
twenty-two, the Mayo Clinic physicians gave me two years
to live. That was over fifty years ago.

Did you ever hear that voice again? The voice that told me my mother would die has been with me all my life during emergencies. It told me when my father would die, when I would change jobs, and more.

How do you apply your talents to health and healing? A woman came to me who was blind in one eye and losing her sight in the other. She didn't have much hope and was suicidal. We tried healing. I held my hands over her eyes. After the fourth treatment, I told her not to fear pain in her eyes. She experienced severe pain there and made an appointment with a specialist. She regained sight in the blind eye. By the time she entered the office, she had perfect vision in both eyes.

Give an illustration of your general psychic abilities rather than your healing abilities. At one time in my life I worked at a California bank, and I often ate at a nearby diner. One evening I saw a woman come through the door, followed by her young son, about thirteen years old. Behind the boy, I saw a spirit, who was his father and the woman's husband. I knew the man had just died.

How did you find out what happened to him? I was very curious, but I certainly couldn't ask. The woman and her son sat down at the counter next to me. The waitress asked her where she had been. She replied that her husband had dropped dead of a heart attack a few weeks ago.

Are there people you've refused to heal? Although healings are what I'm best known for, I don't do them on everyone. Someone once called me for help because her mother had suffered a stroke and a heart attack. I asked how old the woman was. The answer was ninety-eight. I let the old woman go in peace.

Do you believe that events are preordained? I believe that everything is already known if we know how to tune in. We're creating tomorrows by our thoughts today. I've had dreams four and five years in advance of events that turned out exactly like the dreams, so I assume it was already known what was going to happen.

Then do people have a voice in what happens to them? Everyone can have happiness or success because that's a personal thing that you create yourself. Most of the time we attract that which we are. If we're happy and cheerful, we'll attract that kind of person, and if we're down and depressed, we'll bring in a negative force.

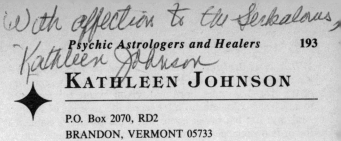

With affection to the Serkalous,
Kathleen Johnson

KATHLEEN JOHNSON

P.O. Box 2070, RD2
BRANDON, VERMONT 05733
(802) 247-3656
FAX: (802) 247-8087

Photo by Tad Merrick

A psychic astrologer, she is known to people mostly through her writings.

What do you like best about being psychic? Doing psychic work makes me feel as if I am an intimate stranger in everyone's life. I get to meet a lot of people, help them, do what I like best—and get paid for it. It's perfect.

What don't you like? People putting down psychics and astrologers. What we say should be just another piece of information to be taken advantage of. There's no reason to make fun of it. But some of the press wants to make us look dizzy or silly. They don't even want us to act sensibly. They want us to come on a program saying, "I don't know what to think. My crystal ball shattered this morning."

What has helped you the most professionally?
Knowing the right people. William Simon, former secretary of the treasury under Ford and Nixon, wrote the foreword to my last book, and he introduced me to a lot of people. And my first big break came when the former Casablanca Records owner became my client, and he introduced me to dozens of people in the music industry, many of whom are still my clients.

What is your background? I was a solitary child. I learned to read at age two and was reading at college level by the time I was four. When I was six years old and in the fourth grade, no one would speak to me because they shied away from too-smart people.

I began high school at eleven and graduated with a 99 average when I was fifteen. I have an IQ over 200. Like most people of my profession, I never graduated from college. I was anxious to live.

How did you get started in the metaphysical realm? From the time I was young, I had vivid dreams as well as funny feelings that came true. At eighteen, I moved to New York to become a singer. Within six years, I became discouraged. That's when I had my astrology chart read and discovered I had an aptitude in that area. At last I had found a way to make being different okay: I started specializing in esoteric astrology, a Tibetan method that charts the path of the soul in each lifetime. I also became an ordained minister.

Are you clairvoyant? Although I am best known for my astrological writings, I am also an analytical clairvoyant. I see with my eyes and I see with my inner eye, and I put the two together.

I often see a movie on the left side of my head. Sometimes there is a voice, but mostly I see pictures. At other times, the information comes to me as if I'm reading a book the size of me, an almost six-foot-tall book, and I'm getting the information from that.

How do you know that what you see is real? I have told enough people what I saw, and they immediately connected it with something. As an example, I saw a picture of a client falling off a horse, and when I told him about it, he told me he was deathly afraid of horses.

As another illustration, I saw a client dressed in Persian garb, and when I told her about it, she told me that she collects seventeenth-century Persian finger bangles. These kinds of things made me believe that what I was seeing was real.

What do you do in the psychic area? I also do readings using tarot, and I teach tarot workshops. I conduct meditation meetings at the new moon for personal healing and at the full one for global healing, because when the moon is full, the light shines everywhere and it's available to everyone.

What have you written in this field? About a million words. Sometimes I do celebrity predictions. For example, I predicted in the *National Enquirer* that Nancy Kerrigan would take the silver medal and Tonya Harding would never skate professionally again. I write for the *Globe, National Enquirer, Armed Forces Network,* and *TV Guide* and have a nationwide cable television show.

KOMAR

323 IHRIG AVENUE
WOOSTER, OHIO 44691
(330) 359-5748
E-MAIL: KOMARR@aol.com

*A psychic healer whose statue is in the
Guinness museums, he has trained
himself to feel no pain.*

***When was the first time you proved to people that
you couldn't feel pain?*** While working on a charity
committee to help the mentally retarded, I set out to prove
that all people are slightly retarded for not using the full
potential of their brain power. I wanted to awaken mankind
to the fact that we have far greater potential than we realize.

Why did you choose to be a human pincushion?
I had to do something spectacular at the show to shock people into paying attention to my message. I knew all people
could relate to pain, and I knew I could turn it off at will.

I thought of the magic of the Hindu fakir of India, who

lies on a bed of nails. I made equipment that I had never tried before on stage. I stripped to a costume under my tuxedo that resembled a maharajah's, and I put on a turban. I jumped up and down with my bare feet on a bed of nails, which, of course, produced blood. I then climbed a ladder of swords made of cane knives. Next, with a couple of torches, I began fire eating. Finally, I lay down on a bed of nails and had two heavy men to jump on top of me.

That must have been pretty dramatic. I wasn't finished. Then I put a second bed of nails on top of me and had four heavy men get on top of that. For the finale, I had someone crush a stone on my chest while I was lying on a bed of nails.

How were you able to do this? I don't have powers unlike anybody else; I've just learned how to focus them a bit better. The mind is only capable of accepting one sensation at a time. Thought is a sensation. Pain is also a sensation. So by outthinking the pain you have none.

In a normal state, I am supersensitive to pain, maybe more so than the normal person. But when I turn it off, I have the ability to throw myself into an altered state of consciousness in which my body produces natural opiates or painkillers and I shut out pain.

During an ABC TV special, a physics professor was trying to debunk me while the show was being filmed. He was still trying when I left for the airport.

Did you develop your psychic abilities or did everything come naturally? When I was nine years old, I found a book entitled *Hindu Yoga Science of Breath*. Without knowing what I was doing, I spent several years developing the concentrative meditate state. I learned the breathing techniques, although I didn't know until I was thirty-one that I was building up my immune system and natural opiates.

I thought I was normal as a child, but I never got any diseases—no chicken pox, measles, mumps. I have not been sick since I started this training at nine years old. Not a headache. Not even a cold.

How do you use your powers? I have done diagnoses, and I did psychic healing for years. I still do predictions when the media call me. It started when UPI called me before Nixon was reelected, and I said he would be reelected but would not finish his term. They asked me if he would die in office. I said, "No, but I see someone else taking over the presidency." I predicted Watergate and didn't even know it!

Many people still consider me to be a great psychic and psychic healer. But some feel uncomfortable around someone connected with the word *psychic*. So I decided to clam up on this psychic bit and work on a "normal" basis. Whatever normal is.

How did you end up in **Guinness?** Following my first show, word spread, and I have been performing ever since throughout the United States, Canada, and over a hundred countries in six continents. I ended up in *Guinness* for two feats: One, which they have since retired, is being a human waffle, sandwiched between two beds of nails with 1,642.5 pounds on top of me. The other is walking on hot coals. There is also a statue of me in all the Guinness museums in the world.

What are a few things people don't know about you? My real name is Vernon Craig. I am married, with three children. I started working at age nine washing dishes in a restaurant, and I have never been out of a job since.

I was a professional baker, and I worked in a cheese factory. I switched to retail and now manage a little Swiss marketplace with cheese and cuckoo clocks here in the middle of conservative Amish country.

I am also a horticulturist. I worked on the landscaping of the College of Wooster. I was in a TV movie with Burt Lancaster. I met Princess Di when I stayed on the estate of her grandmother Barbara Cartland.

How do you care for your body? I do not exercise. I eat anything that tastes good. I smoke, although I tell others not to. I go to bed at two A.M. and get up at six-thirty. I consider myself a "normal" human being. And I am one of the world's most relaxed people. I am sixty-three years old.

IRIS SALTZMAN

INTERNATIONAL PARAPSYCHOLOGY SCHOOL
1899 NORTH EAST 164TH STREET
NORTH MIAMI BEACH, FLORIDA 33162
(305) 944-2781

© 1995 Dianne Collins

Esquire *called her one of the top astrologers in the country, and she's now a psychic astrologer with her own school.*

How do you combine your psychic talents with astrology? Esquire listed me as one of the top fifteen astrologers in the country, but I am really a parapsychologist/ astrologer or a psychic astrologer. For astrology, I use the left side of my brain, the one of the logical world and everyday activities. And for the psychic world, I use the right side of my brain, the visual portion. I use them together, which is supposed to be unique, although I find it natural for me.

When did you realize you were not just an astrologer but a psychic astrologer? When I saw I could do astrology without knowing the person's birthday. Even if they gave me the wrong day, month, and year, I would be able to give them a perfect reading. My psychic ability was correcting the wheel! It really started blowing my mind.

How important is right-brain potential? I believe that primitive people lived in a right-brain world. We think primitive man was backward, but he was really evolved spiritually and could sense or smell danger. He had to tune into his environment if he wanted to survive because he couldn't sit in front of a television set to learn if a hurricane or tornado was coming.

Do we still have the primitive in us? Man has gone too far from his beginning. We're too involved with left-brain activity. I believe everyone has right-brain potential and is psychic—like cats and dogs—they just haven't developed it. I've developed mine more. I call it aerobics of the brain, and I teach it in workshops.

How should people use astrology? People should use their horoscopes as a map, showing them where there are danger spots so they can take a detour. Good astrology is preventive medicine. I think newspaper astrology columns are too general.

How can astrology help people determine their own destiny? For example, children born at the same instant will all have the same ability to carve. One might become a surgeon; a second, a butcher; and the third a murderer. Family influence and abilities play a big role.

What do people learn at your school? I teach them to know themselves through their charts. They have free will to follow it or not. I believe the future is 80 percent destiny and 20 percent free will. I give people tools to work with so they can be their own shrinks. I don't let clients use me or any astrologer or psychic as a crutch.

Give an example of a successful reading. A hotel executive who was also into land development was unhappy with his life and came to me for a psychic reading. I looked at his chart and went beyond it and said, "I see you doing something with medicine, something with doctors." And he said, "What are you talking about? I've never finished high school." But he's now publisher of the main book on alternative medicine! And no more hotel or land work for him.

PSYCHIC ASTROLOGERS AND HEALERS

TERRIE BRILL

POST OFFICE BOX 1771
ELK GROVE, CALIFORNIA 95759
(916) 686-5100
FAX: (916) 686-6373

SUE BURTON

12226 MANOR DRIVE
SOUTHGATE, MICHIGAN 48195
(919) 286-2055

SHARON CAPEHART

17194 PRESTON ROAD, SUITE 123-288
DALLAS, TEXAS 75248
(214) 680-1932

Specialty: Trance channeling

SPENCER GRENDAHL

2265 WESTWOOD BOULEVARD, SUITE 479
LOS ANGELES, CALIFORNIA 90064
(310) 838-6077

JUDI HOFFMAN

165 EAST 89TH STREET
NEW YORK, NEW YORK 10128
(212) 387-0701

CHAPTER

8

Business and Career Psychics

BARBARA COURTNEY

322 MERIDIAN DRIVE
REDWOOD SHORES, CALIFORNIA 94065
(415) 595-4409
FAX: (415) 508-1808
E-MAIL: BAJECO@aol.com

The Dark Room/Debora Cartwright

She's called "The Seer of Silicon Valley," and her clientele is mostly corporate and business people.

What type of questions do business people ask you? How can I be more productive with my group? How can I get along better with someone on the team? How can I tune into others better? What is my future in the company?

And then what do you do? I will tune in and get a sense of how they operate and interact with others. I don't use props like tarot cards. I think there are people who work well with leaves or cards, but those things are limiting to me.

I do not consider myself a fortune-teller. I work much more deeply than that and do not want to be entertainment.

What advice do you give people that they find most helpful? One of the things that gets us into trouble is the pictures in our minds. What we get is what we are willing to accept. It is this resistance to change that keeps us from solving our problems. If we are willing to accept unhappiness and poverty, that's what we get.

Can you give an example? I'll give you a personal one. I once lost fifty pounds quickly, but I still saw myself as a fat person, so I soon gained the weight back. I couldn't stay thin until I saw myself as a thin person.

If we see ourselves as fat, we will be. If we expect others to treat us badly, they will. If we expect love and kindness, that's what we receive. Wishing for changes is not enough. You have to act and believe that what you want is yours. Fake it until you make it is my motto.

Who are your clients? After my two children entered school, I felt there was more to life than the PTA. I returned to the business world to pursue a career in marketing and sales for an electronics firm. Now I see about a thousand clients a year, mostly in the business/corporate world I returned to.

Can you be more specific? My business clients come from firms like Apple, Hewlett-Packard, and IBM. They include CEOs, executives, programmers, financial analysts, and attorneys. Companies that hire me don't always tell their employees that I'm a psychic. They call me their vision consultant.

What is a typical case you've worked on? A man came to me who had been out of work for a while. He had an offer for a job that paid on an hourly basis. He asked me how I felt about his taking it because he didn't think it had any future. And I said, "Some day you'll own the company."

Did he? Sure enough, he went to work there; the parent company had a problem; he had an opportunity to buy it, and within ten years he owned the company.

Have you ever had your psychic abilities studied or tested? A hospital in San Jose, California, Agnew State Hospital, extensively studied and tested brain wave patterns in subjects known to have an unusually high level of intuitive or psychic ability. They were trying to determine if there were differences in patterns with them as compared to others.

What did they do to you? They wired me like for out of space. They put me in this pitch-black room closed off by thick metal doors. It was very terrifying at first; they had lights that flashed inside the room, and they monitored my brain wave patterns.

Did they find something? In the end, they did see some differences in sensitive people like me, but they ran out of money to pursue it further.

What do you think a psychic reading can accomplish for people? I feel there is a tremendous amount of information we can glean from a psychic session because most of us are emotionally involved with our own agendas. We can gain a greater perspective from the detachment that a reading can provide.

It can be difficult for us to see the bigger picture. A reading helps people see a larger picture than they can normally see through their own eyes.

How did you become a professional psychic? I met people who understood these kinds of experiences, and they weren't space cadets. They were doctors and professors. They convinced me that there are dimensions of human reality that some people can tap into and that I had that ability.

Did you start seeing psychics? I went to one who predicted that eventually I'd be a psychic, too. This same psychic overbooked one day and asked me to see two of his clients. I was working in marketing at the time, and after the reading, those two people told people, and they told other people, and it all snowballed.

What is your background? I was born of a family where there was poverty and alcoholism. I was brought up in the southern Methodist "hellfire and damnation" tradition.

My family was constantly moving because my father was a newspaperman, and he kept hoping that the next place was going to be better. I went to fourteen schools in twelve years. I was angry over this and other things, and by the time I was sixteen, I weighed two hundred pounds.

Do you believe in reincarnation? Yes, all that is available to us we are unable to do in one lifetime. After we die, we will live our life over again in a different way, without all our masks.

I believe we will live these lives and deal with things until we get them correct. If we don't learn a particular lesson in one lifetime, we come back to learn it in the next one or the one after that.

Any examples of someone who will come back so they can get it right the next time? I believe someone like Hitler is coming back to revisit this plane because he misused power and will return to correct that.

IMARA

THE WISDOM LIGHT
85 SOUTH UNION BOULEVARD, SUITE G-173
LAKEWOOD, COLORADO 80228
(303) 575-1100

*A former actress and businesswoman,
she is now a business psychic.*

Can you read anyone? I never met anyone I couldn't
read. I've had people come to me and say, "No one can ever
read me." But I can.

Why do you think that's so? Maybe it's because I'm
a skeptic myself. I'm not very trusting, so there is probably
something in me that understands their defense mechanisms
so I can go right in.

Are some people harder to read than others? Of
course. Some people will argue with you. Some want you to
tell them what they want to hear rather than what they need
to hear. If someone puts up a wall, it makes my job difficult,
because first I have to break through it and then I have to
read them.

What is your psychic background? When I was small, I never thought, *I'm psychic.* I come from a Roman Catholic family, and there was no awareness of this kind of thing. So I kept it to myself.

I just thought I was probably adopted and weird. When other kids were doing reports for history on Christopher Columbus, I was doing them on witchcraft in the seventeenth century.

How did you get the name Imara? Imara is the name that was given to me a few years ago through a spiritual experience. Strangely enough, the Japanese tell me it's Japanese, Egyptians say it's from Egypt, Cubans, that it's Cuban, and so on.

Why did you choose to be a business psychic? I'm not an "airy fairy" psychic. I have a business background. I have an undergraduate degree in economics and a graduate degree in business management from one of the top business schools in the country.

Were you in the business world? I used to work as a business executive at Nestlé's, Libby's, and Shasta Beverage. But I burned out after a while and went into my lifelong dream of an acting career.

What is your acting background? I was a bit player and temporary principal actress on *General Hospital* for two summers when Felicia went to France. In addition, I did voice-overs for commercials and was a lead in a movie that was shown in Europe and on video here.

Do you have any theatrical clients? Yes, because of my acting background, I have a lot of celebrity clients. I'm really not at liberty to give out their names. In fact, a lot of my film clients won't even give me their *ages* to put on my records for fear that someone will find out how old they really are.

What type of questions do you answer for your business clients? There are many kinds of business questions that I work with every day: which names clients should choose for companies; what logos or colors work best. Hiring a psychic is a good deal for businesspeople and companies because it would cost a lot more money to hire a consultant or artist to go over these things.

Can you tell the story of someone who came to you with a business question? One client called me about a friend of his with whom he was going to start a restaurant. I told him he would have a real problem with this guy because he was irresponsible. He told me that was impossible, that it was his best friend. He teamed up with the guy and had nothing but problems. Finally, they had to end the partnership. My client lost a lot of money and still doesn't speak to the guy.

Any other examples? A screenwriter came to me for a reading and I told him, "I see this book, and I see the cover in every airport around the country. The way to your success, your riches, your fame, is going to be through novel writing, and through the novel you'll write your screenplay."

Did this please him? He wasn't really thrilled, but the next year he did nothing else but this book. And it wound up in all newspapers as a "record-breaking first-time novel." And *then* he received an offer to write the screenplay. Now he's a multimillionaire. And he got to do his screenplay, with big Hollywood stars and everything.

How do you feel about what you tell people? It doesn't matter what I tell someone if they don't utilize it. Many people make life decisions based on what their psychics tell them, so it's a big responsibility.

We have to become an expert not just on being a good psychic; we have to learn how to communicate or express things appropriately, so that we don't mislead someone or cut off other options for them.

BEVERLY JAEGERS

POST OFFICE BOX 29396
ST. LOUIS, MISSOURI 63126
E-MAIL: info4U@earthlink.net

One of America's best-known business psychics, she also gained fame as a crime psychic. She once received a house as a gift from a client after she made him almost two million dollars.

Is there anything you don't like about having psychic abilities? Yes, everyone wants you to help them find their lost dogs and cats, false teeth, and grandparents' insurance policy. They think you're God. We don't know everything.

Do you call yourself a psychic? I hate the word *psychic*. It gets bad press, and it's often thought of as crazy, crooked, or kooky. I don't think ESP is any stranger than tennis.

I also don't like being called a psychic anymore than I like being called a housewife. If someone asks me if I'm a medium, I always say, "No, I'm an extra large."

Several years ago it was in all the papers that one of your clients bought you a house. How did this happen? In 1974 a man saw me on TV and came to my office with a business question in a sealed envelope. I held the envelope and told him I saw a crop field with red berries on green plants. I saw people, wearing what looked like pajamas, picking the berries. I sensed a crop failure. I saw empty baskets that should have been full. Then Russian tanks and troops came and burned down warehouses.

Did you tell him how these pictures fit together? No, actually I had no idea what I was talking about. But as I talked, I saw the guy was grinning from ear to ear and saying, "Keep going." I found out later that he was a commodities broker, and he was asking me about coffee futures. The two main sources were in Brazil and Angola. He understood that what I was saying was that some would be destroyed by the weather and others through war.

How did you fare? My predictions were on target. He spent $24,000 on coffee futures. By 1976 the price of coffee soared, and his investment grew into 1.8 million dollars.

What did he give you? He asked me what I wanted most. I'd had polio as a kid, and my legs always ached, especially when I walked up and down stairs. So I said, "A house on one floor." He said to go pick one out and he would buy it for me. He gave me enough money to buy a four-bedroom house with a sunken living room and a fireplace and pay the taxes. Pretty good for looking at a sealed envelope. And I hadn't asked for anything in advance!

Have you done any other work with stocks? Several years ago I was in all the papers when a test was conducted to see whether a person with psychic ability could choose better stocks than a stockbroker.

What was the outcome? Nineteen stockbrokers and I were asked to pick five stocks, and I did better than eighteen of the brokers! In fact, sixteen of them chose stocks whose values fell, but mine increased by 17 percent!

Are you still predicting good stocks? These days, although I don't do personal work, I ask my business clients to put the name of a stock on a piece of paper and seal it in an envelope. I hold the envelope and see what it feels like. And then I tell them what I feel.

Do you choose your own stocks? Yes, I've followed my own advice and increased my holdings in the stock market ten times over. But I don't trust my predictions much in commodities. I don't invest in them because your timing has to be exact, and that's the hardest thing in the world to do.

What is the accuracy rate of your psychic predictions? People say I'm almost always right, but I consider any success a miracle because I taught myself to do these things. I don't get help from any other source.

It always puzzled me about those people who say they're in touch with angels or some supernatural source. If so, how come they make mistakes? Those supernatural sources ought to know what they're doing, or why do they bother?

Did you do police work also? Yes, and I think I'm the only crime psychic with a private investigator's license. Thirteen years ago, after I got involved in a case, I was asked by the police to apply for my license because I was handling evidence.

How did you get into that area? My father and grandfather were cops. That helped me, because I knew it was more effective to be affiliated with a police department than to just try and help out as a psychic.

Unlicensed psychics are not allowed to testify, and police departments don't like to work with "citizens" who just call and volunteer information, because they're sometimes flaky.

What is the Psi Squad? I put together a group of licensed intuitive detectives who work on police cases throughout the country. The group is recruited from current and former police officers as well as skilled civilians.

What was the Psi Squad's first case? A missing woman. We were given two personal items of hers. Eventually we found her body in an isolated area. *In Search Of* filmed the case, which is still being shown on TV.

Can you give other examples? We also do cases like the one in which we located a plane missing between Utah and L.A., with a father, mother, and daughter on board. I and two other members of the Psi Squad located the plane twenty-seven miles north of Bakersfield, California, in a very rugged area. Hikers later found it within a mile of our estimation.

What was your most successful criminal case? I worked on the search for a killer who hit a Sacramento, California, 7-Eleven pizza parlor. I kept picking up the initials E.L. and the names Roy and Leonard and a hunting jacket.

Were you on target? Yes, When they found the killer, his name turned out to be Erik Royce Leonard. He was wearing this weird hunting jacket, which was odd in a metropolitan area in California, especially for someone trying to keep a low profile.

What interests you most besides your work? I'm the publisher of *Collectibles Trading Post.* I write columns about cooking and antiques for local publications. I've written twenty-three books, but most are about ESP. I'm also the former publisher of a New Age journal called *Doorway to the Mind.*

Were you always gifted? Not that I realized. When I was twenty-eight, I was working as a journalist. I was preparing an article about the Russians developing ESP abilities in college students. It was the first time I had ever heard of ESP.

How did you get into ESP? I adapted some techniques to test myself. I tried to guess the color of cards turned face down on a table. Or what the mailman would put in my mail. And I played psychic blackjack, that is, played the game without looking at my cards. I found that I was able to do what I attempted.

Then I experimented on my kids, my husband, and friends. When that worked, I got a class together and taught the techniques to strangers. I started out with three people. Eventually I opened my own school, which is now done by correspondence.

Do you think your powers are unique? I don't believe I have any special abilities. I've never found anyone who couldn't learn what I do. I think, though, the higher the intelligence, the better the chance of developing one's ESP.

Do you think it's a gift? I believe it's an ability, not a gift from above. I just fine-tune what we all have. A man will call it a hunch and a woman will call it intuition. Whatever it's called, the world would be a much better place if people would develop what's between their ears.

KATHY REARDON

(804) 741-2404
E-MAIL: 102452.1466@Compuserve.com

Moya Photography

This new mother specializes in career counseling, helping people interested in changing jobs or changing fields.

How do you help people with their careers? I've counseled many people to leave their jobs—if that's what I see is best for them—because that's always a big, scary decision. They know what they have, and they don't know what they're going to get, and they want me to see how they would do if they left their job and often their entire field.

Please give an example. One woman who came to me was a legal secretary and she had been looking for work for a year. And I saw that she was so furious at her previous boss that she was projecting her anger at him in all her interviews.

What did you suggest that she do? I proposed that

she write angry letters to her boss until she got it out of her, then to write a forgiving letter, and then to finally write a really nice letter. After she wrote each letter, she was to burn it. She called me a week later, and she had a job.

Give an example of someone you've helped in a career change. A gentleman who was an entrepreneur and wanted to be a writer came to me. I saw that he should try painting. He was surprised because he had never even considered that as an outlet for his talents. But as the reading started to sink in, over several months, he decided to buy some paints and an easel. He now makes his living as a painter, and his work is sold all over the world.

Other than the fact that many of your clients are unhappy in their jobs, is there anything else that's unique about your clientele? I have a large percentage of first-timers because I seem so normal. I start every reading with a first-time person by telling them that psychic information is never 100 percent accurate. They need to be aware that if they hear something that they think is not right, they should speak up and handle it right then.

Were you more psychically sensitive while you were pregnant? I recently had my first child, a baby girl, at age thirty-seven. During my pregnancy, I could tell that my level of sensitivity went up. I was much more psychically aware, almost annoyingly so.

For example? I couldn't watch the news because whenever there were crime scenes, I was aware of more details than they were presenting. I had to be very selective about what movies I saw or what television shows I watched because I was so psychic it affected me more than usual.

Do you think this is unusual? All parents will tell you that their intuition is heightened when their children are born. But it's especially active in practicing psychics. Still, every mother just knows when her child is in trouble, even when the child is in the other room and she would have no concrete way to tell.

Are your psychic abilities always "on"? Most people's greatest fear when they find out they're talking to a psychic or an intuitive is that you're going to read their minds all the time. Quite honestly, it's not like that. When a car mechanic goes to a shopping mall, he doesn't open up all the hoods of all the cars in the parking lot. It's his day off!

How do you feel when you're "on"? It's exciting and wonderful, when someone walks into the room, to know what's going on with them. But I never discuss these fleeting thoughts with them unless I see that it's something they're very worried about. I then come up with the most tactful way that I can to give them my impressions—without scaring them—especially if they don't know I'm a professional psychic.

How do your parents feel about your being psychic? My parents had no experience with my using my intuitive ability when I was growing up. But they love me as I am now and are supportive. On rare occasions, my mother has asked me important questions, and things have worked out as I said they would.

And your husband? He was raised on the West Coast, where all of this is more commonplace, and he'd been exposed to it before he knew me. He trusts my judgment but leads his own life.

When did you know you had psychic abilities? I first knew it ten years ago when I attended a lecture that labeled my "instincts" as psychic ability. I didn't realize these instincts were psychic at the time, but I relied on them daily.

What about these earlier instincts? Before I went to that lecture, when I was teaching kindergarten, I could sit in the teachers' lounge and know which teachers had a fight with their husbands the night before. And I could tell ten to thirty seconds before a child was about to become very upset.

Did that help you in your teaching? It was helpful because, granted, if you're in a room with thirty small children, you can't always act on your instincts, but you can try to get closer to the child before they do something.

How do you know you're using your psychic abilities and not your reasoning or commonsense skills? I meet a huge percentage of my clientele who call me about jobs only on the phone. I haven't hired a private detective to give me information about their job situations or potential. But I know.

Do you tell them what you immediately know about them? No, I don't always tell them unless they ask because I'm not interested in astounding the world with feats of psychic skill. I'm more interested in helping the person who's calling by answering their questions.

Are you uncomfortable about clients taping your readings? No, I encourage my clients to tape my comments and play them back. Something that is very important frequently turns up, something that I knew in advance, which is a form of precognition.

Do you have a spirit guide? Yes, but I don't use her with everyone. She's an Irish woman named Moira who appeared ten years ago when I entered an altered state. It just happened; I went into a trance. I had done enough reading beforehand so I knew I wasn't blacking out.

Is she always with you? I can use my own psychic ability or I can allow her to come through, so there's a choice. I use my own ability to judge when it is appropriate to let clients know about Moira. If I'm doing a private reading with someone who is comfortable with spirit guides, then she comes through.

What is she like? Moira has a wonderful sense of humor and amazing and accurate things to say to people, and they frequently come true. Over the last ten years, I have learned to trust what she has to say. She has my best interests at heart and the best interests of the people who come to me.

Have you ever considered that Moira might just be another aspect of your own personality? That has been suggested, and I have no way of proving or disproving it. As long as the information is accurate and helpful, people can believe whatever makes them comfortable.

Do you counsel people in areas other than careers? Yes, although career counseling is generally why people call me from all over the country. But I have stockbrokers who are trying to tune into their own market timing; ministers, who, because they spend their time listening to other people, sometimes neglect their own lives, emotions, and challenges; politicians who need help with strategy; doctors who want help in building their business and being better doctors; lawyers for jury selection and case strategy; and people in sales who want to increase their profits.

MORE BUSINESS AND CAREER PSYCHICS

JOAN FRIEL DURHAM

100 VANDERBILT AVENUE
WOODBURY HEIGHTS, NEW JERSEY 08097
(609) 848-4580

PAUL GUERCIO AND "MERLIN" (A COMPUTER)

THE MERLIN PROJECT RESEARCH GROUP
POST OFFICE BOX C
CAMBRIDGE, MASSACHUSETTS 02140
(617) 499-7755
FAX: (508) 388-5961
E-MAIL: merlin@seacoast.com

INGEBORG LILLIE

4410 CARMEN DRIVE
LA MESA, CALIFORNIA 91941
(619) 444-5482

Specialty: Stocks, bonds, and financial analysis

DAVID PEARCE SNYDER

8628 GARFIELD STREET
BETHESDA, MARYLAND 20817
(301) 530-5807

Specialty: Consulting futurist

See: Hy Kaplan and Phyllis Schwartz, page 61.

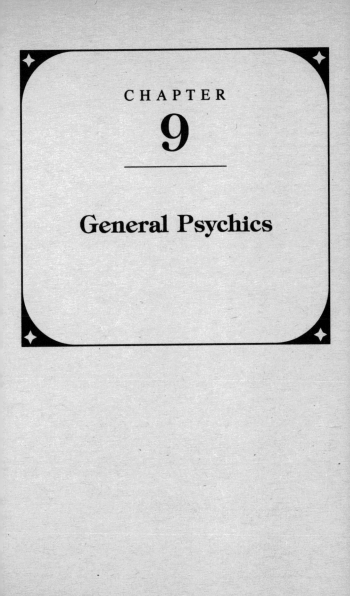

CHAPTER

9

General Psychics

Susan Buchanan

240-12 70TH AVENUE
DOUGLASTON, NEW YORK 11363
(718) 428-5384

Photo by John Hart, NYC

*Sometimes called Ms. Nostra Damus,
she is a clairvoyant consultant.*

What was your best prediction for a client? One
client was a tough cookie with big hair who owned a nail
salon. When I told her she would be engaged or married
within ninety days, she replied that I was crazy. She said
she'd wasted money on a psychic. She was forty and had no
interest in marriage.

What else did you tell her? Although she had never
been out of Queens, except for maybe one trip to Florida,
I saw her in Africa in ninety days married to a man whose
name began with *M* in a town beginning with an *M*.

Did she do anything about your prediction? No,
she ignored me and went back to her work and her three

kids. A month later, a friend who worked for a travel agency invited her to accompany her on an inexpensive trip to the Spanish Riviera. The first day there, my client met a hunk and fell madly in love. They were together for the whole vacation. His name was Miguel. He invited her to take a business trip with him to Marrakech in Morocco. They were married there on a Monday.

Is it dangerous to predict death or illness for a client? Actually, it sometimes almost works against you if you're really good at such predictions because it freaks people out. You want to make a living, but some people get so frightened they don't come back. I only tell them if they are willing to accept such news.

Cite one instance in which this happened. During one reading, someone showed me a picture of her mother, and I grabbed my throat and said, "November." I didn't know what it meant, and she was so unnerved that she didn't return. But eight months later, in November, an intruder broke into the mother's house, robbed her, and slashed her throat.

Presumably, you're glad to give people good news. Of course if something is happy for the person, I tell them. At one party, I ran into a cynic who had been trying to have a baby for four or five years. She was married to a doctor and had been to the best gynecologists available. I told her not to give up, that she would be having fraternal twins, a boy and a girl. She had done in vitro fertilization, which works 20 to 25 percent of the time.

And? She gave birth to a boy and girl the following June. And then I saw *another* pregnancy for her, without in vitro, and I told her she would conceive in July. So she started using birth control. It seemed almost physically impossible that a woman who at one time needed in vitro to conceive now conceived while using birth control. But it happened.

Do you think you were destined to be psychic? I was born with a veil, or thin membrane, over my head. It's a medical condition that's very rare, and there's a superstition that it represents good luck and that the person will be spiritually gifted.

Was yours a difficult background? Most psychics I've met had childhood pain. My mother is a reformed alcoholic, so growing up had its pains. I have also experienced several physical traumas. I was in two automobile accidents, and I have undergone two major operations. After one, in which I almost bled to death, I had a near-death experience. At that point my ESP became very strong.

Was the psychic arena a hobby for you at first? Yes. I married and worked as a stewardess for a division of Pan American Airlines.

As far as I'm concerned, I came from a dysfunctional family and I worked for a dysfunctional company. My division had two crashes in three years, with only six choppers. Statistically, it would be like a major airline having thirty crashes in one year. I quit because I kept seeing these crashes in advance, and it was horrible for me. They eventually went out of business.

That same year, when I was twenty-eight, I also quit my marriage. A friend took me to see a psychic who told me I would be doing this work. Soon, I started visiting psychics every month. Then I started doing this part-time until I got a "real job." But twenty years later, I'm still doing it.

Do past lives play into your readings? Sometimes. Once a woman booked an appointment for three people. She came in first, while the others with her waited outside. I saw her in the South in the 1800s. She was married to the same man she is married to now. I saw that he had only one eye. She had no reaction to my reading. When she left, the next person walked in. It was her husband. His eyes looked normal. I told him what I had told his wife. He revealed that he was wearing a glass eye.

What is your religious background? I was raised a Catholic but became an agnostic as a teenager. Later, I became a born-again Christian of the Protestant faith, and now I'm a student of the Jewish cabala because that's what Christ studied.

I believe that the Catholic saints and their counterparts in other religions are all really superpsychics.

LITANY BURNS

POST OFFICE BOX 776
NYACK, NEW YORK 10960

Ron Rinaldi

*She has read for European royalty and
celebrities like Madonna and helped
identify the Son of Sam.*

Do you enjoy being psychic? Sometimes it can be
frustrating. If you tell somebody that you're a writer, no one
asks you to write something on the spot. But if you tell
someone you're a psychic, they immediately ask you some
question or try to make you prove yourself to them in
some way.

Why do you think people should go to psychics?
Psychics can help people get more in touch with their own
abilities. They can also help them choose more wisely in
personal relationships and help them with other decisions,
whether it's selecting a date, a plumber, a babysitter, or a
stock.

Psychics can help people cut to the chase. They can help someone be less likely to get caught up in a relationship that's bad or buy a lemon.

Do clients generally take your advice? I'll give you an example of someone who didn't. A French producer came to see me about a side business venture. He wanted to open an exclusive restaurant with several partners. He gave me letters to hold with the signatures of his potential partners.

I told him in great detail the problems he would personally have with each of his partners in this venture. He also gave me the name of the restaurant written on a piece of paper, and I held it and told him I felt he should not invest in it. I later heard he invested three hundred fifty thousand dollars and the restaurant never opened. He lost all of his money.

What did you see in the Son of Sam case? The Son of Sam was a madman who terrorized the outer boroughs of New York City by shooting beautiful women, most of them long-haired brunettes. They were generally in deserted places, sometimes with their boyfriends, often in a car.

Near the end of the killings, I was called in by the D.A.'s office. I used psychometry and held on to a private letter written to journalist Jimmy Breslin from someone who called himself "Son of Sam."

I was able to tell that the killer was adopted, that one of his biological parents had died, that he worked in a post office in the Bronx, that there would be another killing, and that there would be an eyewitness; also that soon after that final killing, he would be apprehended for something that had nothing to do with the case. These predictions came true, and David Berkowitz was picked up because of a parking ticket he got in an area near the last shooting.

What was the most unusual situation in which you were asked for advice? When I first started reading, a woman I knew nothing about told me she was involved in a lawsuit. She wanted to know if she was going to win because all her money was tied up in it.

I saw this small man with a mustache and bald head in a desert area, and I told her that something bad was going to happen to him. I told her that she would get some of her money back, and the man was going to be exposed. On her way out, I asked her, "By the way, who are you suing?" She said, "I'm suing the shah of Iran!" Of course, a few years later, he was exposed and ousted. I assume she got some of her money back.

Do you remember the first time you were fascinated by something psychic? When I was twelve, a "country" kid from upstate New York, my family and I went to New York City and visited a big toy store. I was told I could buy only one toy. I was drawn to a Ouija board, although I had no idea what it was. I kept going back to it and looking at it, trying to figure out what it was. I wound up buying it. At home with the Ouija board, I immediately started talking to a spirit. I've been talking to him ever since. He is my oldest and dearest friend, and we have helped a lot of people together.

Whom do you read for now? I've read for everyone right up to royalty—an Italian prince and a British duchess—and even Madonna, who I read for twice in the early 90s.

Do you also do healing? Yes, like the time a seventy-year-old woman client was having open-heart surgery. Her daughter called me at her mother's request and asked me if I would send her healing energy at a specific time on the day when she was having the operation 150 miles away.

I focused on sending that energy then and soon heard her mother's voice in my head. She told me she had left her body and was happily visiting with her deceased husband. I urged her to return to her body on the operating table immediately because I felt her daughter was very distraught and worried about her.

Were you later able to verify this experience? When I later spoke with her daughter and told her what I saw, she was speechless. Her mother's heart had stopped beating at exactly the time I was communicating with her, and the doctors had trouble reviving her. They were about to pronounce her dead when her heart began beating on its own.

What happened? She survived the operation and lived for many more years.

Emma Facciolo

STATEN ISLAND, NEW YORK
(718) 494-2886

Expressly Portraits

*She does mostly phone readings and
has the sign of the psychic in her hair.*

***How did you know you were different from
others?*** I looked different. When I was about nine, I moved
into a new home. I went to sleep for the first time in my new
bed, and very a weird sensation came over my body. I could
not move. The next day I woke up, and I had a white streak
in my hair. And I've had it since that day. It does not take
color. Nothing changes it. It's been with me since then.
Some believe that it is the sign of a true psychic. But in other
ways, too, I always knew I was different from other people.

How did you feel about being different? I thought
I was a little bit crazy. As a child, I hid it and didn't really
act on anything. I always knew things without putting a name
to it. I was always fascinated by the unknown.

Did you ever dream of anything that came true?
I'm an only child, and my mother and I were very close and
never fought. More than twenty years ago I had a dream. In
the dream, my mother and I fought. She stabbed me in the
hand with scissors, and it started to bleed. I kept running in
panic and found myself in what must have been purgatory.

I woke up with the most horrible headache. I was terrified
and could not move from my bed. I told my mother of my
dream. She was very upset, and I cried all day. I knew something terrible was going to happen.

The next day, my mother, who seemed to be in the best
of health, suffered a cerebral hemorrhage and died three
days later. I saw it happen in front of me. I later went to a
psychic to help me understand it.

*When did you first do something publicly with
your powers?* After my mother's death, I was at a party.
There was a nurse there, and it came out of my mouth that
she was having an affair with her doctor, who was married.
She was stunned! She got very angry afterward with the
hostess and said, "How dare you tell her my private life!"
Of course, she had not told me anything. After that, I was
frightened. Where was this information coming from? I
didn't want to be what people thought of psychics—a flake
with lots of makeup and gold earrings.

Where does your information come from? Sometimes I get a vision and actually see the house or the person
I'm talking about. I don't go into trances. I guess I use my
psychic abilities when I watch mysteries on TV because I
immediately know who did it. I believe my gift comes to me
from God. When I start a reading, I say a prayer and ask
for guidance from God.

How do you conduct your sessions? I won't do
readings if I'm tired. I have to feel personally strong. I did
not do readings when I menstruated because I didn't want
to incorporate any irritability or negativity into the reading.

Have you ever lied during a reading? If I don't feel I
have an answer to your question now, I'll say I'm not getting
anything on it. I've learned that people appreciate my
honesty.

I also learned my lesson about lying a long time ago when

I was very new. A woman was looking for a job, and just to make her feel better, I told her, "I see you getting a job at such and such a time." She never got the job. I told her later I was wrong and wrong to tell her. Total honesty is important, I know now.

Do you start work on a client before the actual session? When someone calls, all I need is her name, who referred her, and her date of birth. We make an appointment for a phone or personal reading. Before her reading, I sit down and meditate.

I use a religious candle; Saint Jude, who is the saint for hopeless and impossible causes; and a white candle for purity to keep down negativity. I say a prayer for guidance from the Lord, and I ask that the person know no more or no less than she is supposed to know at this time in her life. I pray that only God's light will come into this reading.

I take the paper with her name and her date of birth, and I write down her sign and the four major things that I think are the most important things for everyone: health, love, money, career. I concentrate on each thing and I write down on each subject whatever comes through.

When I read for the person, we go over what I have written, and I add her personality traits. My clients are flabbergasted each time.

How accurate are you? I'm not God. I can be wrong. I don't want to rule anyone's life. I don't want people to become dependent on me. I give them advice, and then it's up to them.

Did you ever do free readings? When I started, I didn't ask for money, but people think you sit home all day long at your phone and they call you at all hours to help them with their problems. I have a family to raise, so I started to charge. But if people are having financial difficulties, I still don't charge them.

Do you take anyone who calls you? You have to be careful because people are searching and may believe anything they are told. If someone is sick, I tell him to pray or to search for professional help. I'm a psychic; I'm not a psychiatrist. I'll tell him he may need medical help.

One woman called me for an immediate reading a few

months ago. I picked up paranoia, and I told her, "I can't help you, but I advise you to get help immediately." The next day she signed herself into a hospital and got treated, and she's better.

Give an example of someone who didn't take your advice. A girl came to me. I told her the relationship with her boyfriend would never work out. She married the man. A month later she came back to me. He had abused her. She divorced him. She told me the marriage was something she had to do even though I had advised her against it.

Knowing you are psychic, does your family take your advice? My daughter went out with a man for ten years. When the time came for them to marry, I told her, "Don't do it." She did it anyway, and she was back home in less than a year.

SHEILAA HITE

23852 PACIFIC COAST HIGHWAY, SUITE 126
MALIBU, CALIFORNIA 90265
FAX: (310) 589-5449

Photo by Alan Ascher

*A psychic intuitive, she has done
everything from ghost busting to love
counseling to helping people get over
stage fright.*

What is your most unusual case? I once talked a
woman whom I didn't know out of suicide. She called me,
wouldn't give me her last name or phone number, and said,
"As soon as we're done talking, I'm going to kill myself."

Did she tell you why? She was at the end of a bad
relationship, and nothing had ever worked out for her. For
two hours I chose to work with her, and whatever I said
showed her that one person in this world cared about her
and thought she was of value and worth saving. I got her
assurance that she wouldn't kill herself and asked her to call
me the next day.

Did she? She called to thank me and said she saw the world in a different way. I referred her to a therapist. I never did get paid. I love money and it does wonderful things, but you can't really say to a suicide: "By the way, do you have any money?"

Describe a haunted house you've been in. Recently, for *The Other Side,* I spent a night in a haunted inn in Gettysburg, Pennsylvania. The place had been used as a hospital and amputorium, and I felt a lot of pain and agony. As I went through the place, I felt strong presences of soldiers killed during the Battle of Gettysburg.

In the cluttered attic was the most negative energy. I saw a young, confused Confederate soldier in the corner. He was badly wounded and had died slowly and painfully for a cause he did not understand.

Were you scared? That night, when I went to my bedroom, I left the light on. I didn't want to go to sleep. I kept telling myself that I was a brave person and that I must experience sleep, but I barely slept. At five-thirty in the morning, I heard heavy footsteps between my room and the one next to me. I had left the light on, but somehow it got turned off—I don't believe that happened naturally.

Were you able to change the energy in the place? Later, I saw that the attic contained the original wood of the 1800s, which attracts spirits. I said they should sort through the old relics and clear the space up there, and when they did that, the energy changed.

How have you helped people handle stage fright? I've assisted many adults and students through exams and auditions and also helped the singer and songwriter Riva Hunter, who developed stage fright and started forgetting lyrics. Through guided imagery, I gave her the tools to get past her blocks and fears and adapt to situations. She has since gone on to heal her life and create the situations she desires.

How do you help people having relationship problems? I can't solve the problems in relationships—that's up to the couple—but I can give people a different perspective and information that isn't readily available to them. Then they can make their own decisions about what to do.

I also have therapists I work with—I feel psychics and therapists should work together—and I send clients to those who are sympathetic to the fact that the person is sensitive enough to seek out a psychic.

When did you become professional? I had been reluctant throughout my life to fully employ my intuitive skills, although I had used them throughout the years for extra money or as a favor to friends. But in 1988 I became full-time. I began working the fairs in Santa Monica, and in Malibu I worked at the Malibu Shaman Book Store, where I still work on Saturdays.

I have also worked and studied in India; Montevideo, Uruguay; Malaysia, Hawaii, New Orleans, and New Mexico. Wherever I go, I wind up working, although I don't travel to work.

What did you do before? Careerwise, I designed and manufactured clothing, and I was a costumer for television and films. I've worked on *Hill Street Blues, Blade Runner, and Alfred Hitchcock Presents,* the new series. I have also been a waitress, an accountant, and a business manager.

What methods do you use? Since I am psychic, I can work without tools, but at different times I use tarot, astrology, psychometry, palmistry, dream interpretation, channeling, meditation, healing, and hypnotherapy. I've done work with past lives, but I believe the one that you are living now is the most important. You want to look at and see what's going on here.

JOYCE KELLER

BOX 78
WEST ISLIP, NEW YORK 11795
PHONE AND FAX (516) 587-2013

Jack Keller

*She hosts the longest-running live
psychic TV and radio show in America.*

***What's the hardest thing about doing private
psychic readings?*** People who come to see psychics
are often out-of-work people with no income, wives whose
husbands are ill, women who are going through divorces or
other painful transitions, and have very little money. I can't
take money from them because they don't have it.

Another problem with private readings is that we are short
of men in our society. Many women go to psychics to find
out how they can get their married boyfriends to leave their
wives. It becomes very discouraging. So many women are
dating married men, patiently waiting for them to leave their
wives. They want me to tell them when it will happen. But
will it really happen? In most cases, no. I cannot lie and tell

them it will happen and then take money. So I don't get involved in these kinds of cases.

Besides reading for a select clientele, what do you do? I do community service radio and TV shows, guest appearances on radio and TV, freelance writing, and lecturing.

How did you get into media work? I started teaching yoga in my twenties. Then I went to college, got married, and had two children. I began my television show called *Trim and Slim*. In it, I gave readings to telephone callers.

I saw that TV put me in the position of being there for people needing help. That show led to the TV and radio shows I host today.

I was able to carve out a niche for myself in the media because I am a certified hypnotherapist and my specialties are relationships, past-life regression, dream analysis, astrology, handwriting analysis, grief therapy, and death preparation.

Give an example of the type of advice you give people on radio. A woman called me: "My father has Alzheimer's disease, and he's missing." I psychically picked up that he was in Florida. But it didn't feel tropical. I felt it was someplace having to do with transportation and that he was sitting there waiting.

Did she find him? Later, she told her husband what I said. He reminded her that her father had old cronies living in a small town upstate. They got in their car and found her father sitting in the bus terminal in Florida, New York. No wonder I didn't see palm trees.

Were you brought up among psychics? My mother was a psychic who could read anything. She was a great cook and read spaghetti stuck to the bottom of the pot. She could read string beans on a dish the way other people read tea leaves! The woman was totally psychic—and I thought this was normal! She was an astrologer, and instead of teaching me to read *Run, Spot, Run*, we would spend time analyzing dreams and looking them up in a dream book.

Did others appreciate your burgeoning psychic abilities? When I started school, I thought this was all terribly normal. So the first day in kindergarten, I raised my hand and told the teacher, "You have to go home now. Your mommy is very sick." She told me, "I don't want any more outbursts from you. I want you to be quiet the rest of the day." But the next day she came in with a completely different attitude toward me. She knelt by my side, took my hand, and asked, "How did you know my mother was ill? She went to the hospital yesterday." She had new respect for me!

Did you speak out after that? No, I realized you cannot just share messages without repercussions. There has to be discretion in the delivery of the message. By the time I was in first grade, I could cover my psychic abilities over completely, and people I went to school with didn't have a hint. I killed off a lot of the psychic ability I had already developed. I cut off past-life memories and invisible playmates. All that was shoved under a rug until I needed it years later.

Dr. Gerri Leigh

741 WEST END AVENUE, SUITE 1F
NEW YORK, NEW YORK 10025
(212) 316-1619

*She does some unusual things, like
suggesting love potions and doing what
she jokingly calls "nostrology."*

**How did things change for you once you became
successful?** When I first started out, I would ask people
to bring a ring or watch or anything of value so I could get
something that was intrinsically important to them. But they
thought maybe I was going to rob them. So now they trust
me, especially after the *New York Times* did a big story
on me.

**Have you ever worried what people thought
about your being a psychic?** At first, when I was
asked to do all these radio and television shows, I didn't
really want to because I didn't want anyone to know. I

thought that once they saw me, they'd think, *How could people take me home to their parents?*

Did you tell people what you did? When people asked, I had trouble saying this was my profession. I would say, "Well, I have to work now." It's funny because now I've been referred to as "the psychic you can bring home to Mom." Actually, my mom used to think I was crazy.

How did your being psychic upset your parents? When I was two years old, I was running a terrible fever, and I said, "Vishnu has come to save me, Mommy. He is on my bed." And I described him as having "a kerchief around his head like an Indian."

Were they alarmed by this? My mother asked my father if he was watching *Ali Baba* or a show like that and he said no. My mother was really worried about me. When I was older, I found out Vishnu was a preserver. He was hovering over my bed like a pendulum, saying, "I am Vishnu. I am here to protect and preserve you and make you well."

Do you have any other early psychic memories? I also remember floating over my bed and up to the ceiling and just describing what was up there. I was just a little girl and that kind of freaked my parents out.

Since I couldn't tell my mother about these things, I told my grandmother, and we became very close. I still have access to her even though she is no longer on this plane. She tells me what ingredients to put in any dish I want to make. That way I don't have to buy expensive cookbooks.

What can you read? Hair, nails, faces, feet, walls—anything, provided it's not too kinky. I have read Morton Downey's cigarette butts. I also do crystal gazing, read people's photos, and do pet telepathy. I read Geraldo Rivera's dog hair and correctly predicted he would move into a new home and get involved in the martial arts again.

What is nostrology? I introduced what I jokingly called "nostrology" on Geraldo's show when I predicted who the next president would be, based on what the candidates' nostrils looked like. Later I read Jerry Springer's nostrils and correctly detected his true love and talent for singing country music.

What else? I can also affect living things psychically. For example, I get rid of vermin in a house or apartment by making a mental pact with the bugs. "If you come here, you die, so go somewhere else." And they do!

Have your methods changed over the years? People come to me with questions and pictures in addition to objects, and I try to do a combination platter of what I feel like doing and what they want to know. I might read their palm or do tarot, astrology, psychometry, numerology, or Cabala, or all.

Also, although now I use a little of everything, when I did readings at first, I didn't like tarot cards and astrology because it was outside me. I only liked dreams or things that were inside. The other things felt gypsylike or weird, and I didn't want people to think I was crazy. I wanted to hide my ability as much as possible.

Is there anything you don't do? I'm asked for but won't give help in numbers for the lottery. I cannot misuse these gifts—although I made an exception once when my mother called from Las Vegas and asked for a couple of roulette numbers.

If you see that someone will die, do you tell them? No, even though I do sometimes see it when I read palms. A woman came to me and said, "No one will read my palm. Every time someone reads my palm they just put it down." So I looked at her palm and saw a massive stroke and instant death. Of course I wasn't going to say that. So I asked her, "Do you want to live?" And she said, "That bad, huh?"

What did you tell her then? I told her she had high blood pressure, drank too much coffee, had a volatile temper—which turned out to be true—and this all had to change if she wanted to live. Since I couldn't really give her medical advice, I told her statistically what works: Cut down on salt, stress, nicotine, and caffeine; exercise; eat garlic; and check with her doctor.

What are your feelings about channeling? I only do it for friends because to do it I have to lie down and go into a semisleep state.

I have found that people in New York use channelers for

different reasons than elsewhere in the country. I used to live in Los Angeles. People there want channelers to tell them the meaning of life and why they're on this planet, what their mission is.

What do they want to know in New York? They're very practical. For example, New Yorkers have asked me to predict the plays in a Giants game or give tips on the stock market, on getting a cheap apartment, a parking space, or a summer home in the Hamptons. And people from Maine and Minnesota call me asking where they can catch fish!

Who do you usually channel? I have channeled stars like Greta Garbo, but most of the time I have regular channelers, like Manuela, a Spanish psychic who's very earthy, so I have to edit out a lot of her words or I'd have people leaving here crying.

What do you mean? Someone comes to me for a reading and suddenly I hear Manuela saying, "She ought to dump the creep." I'm not going to make this woman have a nervous breakdown, so I say to her, "It probably would be wise not to put all your eggs in one basket at this time. I don't get the sense that he's the one who's going to take you to your next step."

Have you ever suggested a love potion for your clients? Sometimes I do to help maintain relationships or bring people mates. But it doesn't always work the way you think it will. I gave one woman a potion and a ritual to do to bring her true love. A month later she said, "It's great. I'm dating like crazy, but all the men are married." When I asked her what she was requesting from the universe, she said, "I asked the Divine Mind to bring me a husband." Well, that's what he brought her. She should have asked for *her* husband. She finally did it right and met someone.

What did you do before you were a professional? I started out in my late teens as a talent coordinator for Joe Franklin. (I told him later that his future was a thing of the past!) I was also a singer, an actress, and a model and had a sideline talent agency in which I booked singers and bands. Then I got into production, producing commercials and scripts, and next I produced game shows, which is how I wound up in California.

What did you do in the psychic area in California? I had gotten a masters in psychology from Baruch College, and then I got a doctorate in parapsychology. I developed this thing call Astropath, a birth chart translator, to prove astrology was baloney. But it always ended up to be right.

What did you do with Astropath? I sold it through mail order just to make money. It was a mercenary thing at first because I didn't want to live in my parents' basement forever. But I was invited to parties from the advertising agencies, and I was reading people's palms. I ended up writing a book about it.

What is your philosophy? I believe that if you can have a good laugh, you can have a good life. When you can't laugh and you're in a tizzy, pray. Turn things over to God. Life is eternal. There is no real death. I found that out because I can communicate with people on the other side.

BETTY LIPTON

INNER VISIONS PSYCHIC CENTER
1 MIDDLE STREET
PORTSMOUTH, NEW HAMPSHIRE 03801
(603) 436-2412
FAX: (603) 431-8062

Brandon McDaniel

*This psychic became known as a
witch—even though she never was one.*

How did you get known as a witch? At seventeen
or eighteen, I was a real flower child. I went to this Grateful
Dead concert in 1969, and the tickets were all sold out. So
I went to the door and said, "I'm a witch, let me in."

They said the only place I could go was backstage to hang
out with everyone and party. So I did that, and everyone's
passing drinks around—who knew what was in them? And
then they said to me, "To prove that you're a witch, you
have to give a reading to Jerry Garcia."

What did you tell him? Jerry put his hand out, and I
touched it and said, "Jerry, your band is going to be trucking

even when you're an older man." And he said, "I like this girl." So he took me out on stage during the whole concert, and I danced. I got written up in the Grateful Dead book as the "good witch from the East Village" even though it wasn't true.

What was the progression of your metaphysical life? My mother was psychic, and one day when I was about ten, she took my hand and began to explain to me what the lines on my hand meant. All of a sudden I got this psychic feeling about what the other lines there meant. I started saying, "This is going to happen, and this is going to happen." And everything that I said was either true then or became true later.

Did you continue in the psychic path? I started reading palms in school, and all the kids were coming to me on the lunch lines for a reading. Instead of saying hello and waving at me, they were putting their hands in my face.

At first, I really liked having the ability to be psychic. I think I also liked people to like me for it, too. But then, when I got older, around seventeen, people were coming to me left and right for palm readings. I said to myself, "Wait a minute. This is really a gift from God, and I ought to start charging, or people won't appreciate it and will take advantage of me."

It's this karmic thing, like an exchange. So I charged and did parties and coffeehouses, beginning at seventeen. I'd give people my card, which had my eyes on the card as a logo.

How did you become a professional psychic? I began by reading out of my mother's antique shop, and I also co-owned a well-known metaphysical bookshop called The Witches Brew in Portsmouth, New Hampshire.

Now I have a very large clientele all over the country from word of mouth. I have my own office at an executive center and I don't even have a sign outside. People just come.

What do you do for them? I do tarot, palm reading, touch vibrations, and psychometry. I am clairaudient and clairvoyant. It's not like a photograph; it's more like a negative. I'm also a medium. I can get messages from anyone who has passed on for a couple of years.

***What is the strangest thing that's happened to
you psychically?*** My brother Joey, this wonderful, incredible man, was sent to Vietnam in 1967. When he left, he
told the family, "You know, I'm not coming back!"

I was very connected to him, and he promised me as he
left—and it was one of those very strong vows: "If any man
ever hurts you, I'll come back."

As soon as he got to Vietnam, he got sick and was evacu-
ated in a helicopter. The helicopter was shot down. Even
before we were notified, he told me in a dream that he had
died, and he came back to me many times again in my
later dreams.

Then what happened? A year later, I was in Greenwich
Village, and this well-dressed man came over to me. "I'm
looking for this particular address," he said. Well, I have a
very good heart and I wanted to help him, so I went with
him when he asked me to show him where it was.

He lured me into an alleyway and grabbed me. He put his
hands around my throat and told me to get undressed. I said,
"Take my money," and then I screamed really loud. And he
said, "If you scream one more time, I'll kill you."

You must have been terrified. What did you do?
The second time I screamed only in my mind: *Joey!* And all
of a sudden a building door opened, and I saw an arm directly
smash this man in the face. And the blood started pouring
from my would-be rapist's nose, and he took off down the
block.

Afterward I saw another guy staggering nearby. He was
weak, a drug addict. And I said, "Thank you, you saved me."
And he said, "Hey, lady, get away from me. I heard you
scream. I didn't have any reason to save you. But the second
time you screamed, that was some spooky stuff. I felt my
whole body being whisked up in the air and blown across
the street. Get away from me."

I believe my brother took over the body of this weakened
addict and kept his vow to protect me.

Llorraine Neithardt

NEW YORK, NEW YORK
(212) 757-8914

Horhai Ocheo

*This visionary says her readings are
"conversations with the soul."*

How do you help your clients? I deal in personal
disasters, not natural ones. But rather than get involved in
the prediction of a disaster in one's life—which could or
couldn't happen—I try to change a person's way of thinking
and being, so that if the disaster does occur, it has meaning.

What do you do to accomplish this? I try to use
common sense with people and not guide them into such
abstractions that their whole everyday lives start to collapse.
People have more inner resources to handle crises than they
realize because when something bad happens, their lives
don't fall apart, they just kind of break into these different
pieces to be reordered.

Do you tell people what to do? No, I let them make up their own minds. A woman came to me, and I saw that there was a great likelihood that her mother would not live through Christmas. I suggested that her mother was in an ending cycle and that she might want to stay with her during the holidays. The choice was totally hers.

What did she do? She decided to go out of town, and her mother passed on. And she came back to me crying and asking why hadn't she seen what I was saying. That's because in the reading, I suggest. I don't give an absolute, since free will and noninterference is the law of the cosmos.

Do you tape-record readings? I tape for clients and encourage them to replay the tapes even years later. I'm not concerned about being right or wrong. I'm concerned about what events mean to them and to the depths of their being or their souls. Sessions are like poetry. When they hear them at different points and at different levels, there are deeper meanings.

What system do you use? I don't have a particular method. My particular expertise is in working with the soul. It's forty-five minutes for your soul to talk. When the soul presents to me what the problem is, then I have the guidance of higher forces—my readings are like faxed questions of God—and boom, something happens, a shift occurs in the person.

And? Suddenly they have an understanding or the beginning of an understanding of something they didn't have before. I don't care if they're skeptical at first, because you can believe or not believe in electricity, but you get shocked if you stick your finger in that socket.

Do you use any tools? Sometimes I use cards because then the person doesn't become preoccupied with "Where the hell is she coming up with this stuff from?" It's easier to blame it on the cards. I also use information astrologically so that I can know the right language to talk to them. You can't talk to a Virgo the way you talk to an Aquarian. They're not the same, and they hear things in a different manner. I used to use Druid runes, which are pieces of oak bark that one can use to make predictions. But this is just a focus for the mind. People use shells, rocks, and tea leaves.

How do your readings change people's lives?
Once I designed clothes, but now I design and seed the divine design within people. Instead of being a shoemaker, I became a soulmaker, and I mirror the deepest part of their being, the motivating force behind it all, the parts they cannot get to. I kind of get in there and pull out the *real* sludge.

How? When people come to me, they need to have meaning to this darkness, because we can suffer anything if it has meaning. I go into the darkest part of people because that's where the divine lives, and once they become aware of that, they can start making tremendous changes. Otherwise, what we don't know about ourselves will return to us and get us into trouble.

When did you first realize that you perceived things differently from others? Throughout my childhood, I saw beings who were always with me and guided me. But it was only gradually that I became aware that I perceive differently from others.

In my teenage years when everyone began to take drugs, friends would tell me they would see, hear, and know things and colors. And I became terrified because I was seeing things and hearing and knowing without taking anything. I probably was more terrified that drugs would make me more normal than anything else!

Did you ever have a near-death experience? Two. The first time was in my early twenties. I was just graduating from the Parsons School of Design, and I had gotten near to death because of anorexia, which is a disease that has to do with spirit and how you perceive yourself. I wound up in the hospital and went through the classic near-death experience.

How did that change you? It was after that I decided to go to a psychic. She went on about my gifts and things that were going to happen, and I thought she was quite mad. And I found out later *I* was mad and *she* was absolutely fine.

Did you visit more psychics? Although I was in Freudian analysis, I visited an astrologer, and a whole world opened up to me. I found a language for my soul to live in. I began to study astrology and I kept designing, but now my clients were staying hours and hours, because I was telling them things about themselves and they were starting to feel better.

And I still was not catching on that that was my real work. I didn't totally surrender to all the weird stuff like Druid divination and Bach remedies, which are remedies made from flowers, until later.

When did you become professional? After a serious accident resulting in my second near-death experience, I realized I was being stalked by the divine. And then one day I saw a bag lady, and my heart said, "I think she's an angel." There was just something about her. She had a great sense of style. She asked me for money, and I thought, *Today is as good a day as any to die,* and I gave her my last cent, which was $1.67. And then I thought, *I'll go home to kill myself.* When I got home, the phone rang and someone said, "I hear you're an extraordinary psychic and visionary. How much do you charge for a reading?" So I said, "I don't know— thirty-five dollars?" And I've been working ever since.

Barbara Norcross

235 SUNRISE AVENUE
PALM BEACH, FLORIDA 33480
(407) 655-4413
(213) 851-9193

The only licensed psychic in Palm Beach, Florida, this all-around psychic was called in on the William Kennedy Smith rape case.

Do you use any props? As far as I'm concerned, crystal balls, Ouija boards, black cats, and Friday the thirteenth are Halloween stuff. I'm not a fortune-teller. I don't speak to the dead. I "hear" some things and "see" others. And I don't levitate anything but me.

What did you do before you were a psychic? I've had a colorful life. One of my husbands turned out to be a gangster and not the businessman he told me he was. Another gave me a yacht as a wedding present. After our honeymoon, he disappeared for a year. Then he returned—and took the yacht!

What kind of jobs have you had? I was once a veterinary assistant. A dog groomer. A professional entertainer signed with the William Morris agency. I owned and managed two nightclubs in Texas. I was an antique store assistant.

Several years ago I was an executive chef in El Paso, Texas. I was so inundated by work that one day I asked myself, "Oh, God, how much longer do I have to do this?" That day I fell and hit stainless steel on my way down and was severely injured.

I had to learn how to walk again, and I regrouped my whole life in the seven years of surgeries and relearning how to walk and be mobile. That's when I realized that I wasn't meant to do that, and I had the time to dedicate myself to my psychic studies. I think God tells you things.

Were there any other incidents that changed your perception of yourself or the world? Later, when I was married to a military man and we were living in Germany after the war, I visited Dachau, the Nazi concentration camp, and went into the shower room where the Nazis had gassed prisoners. When I stepped inside, I could hear every voice of every person who ever crossed over there. I lost it. I woke up hours later in an infirmary on a military base where my family had taken me after I collapsed. After that I simply couldn't ignore my psychic abilities.

Give some examples of these abilities. For example, I advised a mother not to let her son accept a ride on a particular day. Two days later, the mother called to tell me some friends had offered her son a ride, but he had turned it down at her insistence. All the kids in that car were killed right after they drove away.

Other instances? A lady called me to say she had lost two gold rings. I saw a carpet and asked her if someone she knew had carpet installed recently. Several days later she called me back to say the rings were found under her daughter's new carpet.

What about the Kennedy case? When I moved to

Palm Beach in 1991, as soon as I got there, I knew something was coming down with a politician in town. Then the William Kennedy Smith scandal broke. I was called in twice by one of the investigators.

What did you tell them? If I told you, I would never be asked to work on another case by them.

How do you feel about your special ability? It's a gift from God, and I want anyone who needs a reading to be able to afford it. I've done many readings for free.

I've turned down large fees because I believe my gift must be shared. Otherwise it will be lost. As long as I use my gift to benefit others, I'll have it.

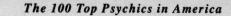

BEATRICE RICH

14 HORATIO STREET
NEW YORK, NEW YORK 10014
(212) 989-1339

Jamie Robinson

Once a full-time humanities professor, she became a professional psychic at thirty-seven.

What's the best thing a magazine or newspaper has said about you? One of my clients was quoted in a magazine as saying about me: "I don't care if she calls herself a psychic, analyst, or a chopped liver sandwich. For me she has been 85 percent on target, and that's a better percentage than many of the economists and stock analysts on Wall Street."

What is your favorite success story concerning your use of psychometry? Once, at a party of about forty people, I was given an envelope with a large pearl ring set in gold. I tried it on, felt the vibrations, and looked through the audience for the hand to match the ring. I correctly identified the woman.

Do certain objects work better for psychometry?
I ask people to bring an object, such as jewelry, a pen, or a lipstick, to their session. The item cannot be an antique, an heirloom, a gift, or anything owned by anyone else or that they've loaned to someone else. They had to have bought it for themselves, and it must have been in their possession for at least one month, although the longer they've owned it the better. Also, it can't be a handmade object because then I might be picking up on the person who made it rather than the one it belongs to.

Do you use anything in addition to psychometry? I almost always use a regular deck of playing cards as a catalyst to begin the process of ascertaining information. The cards themselves have no intrinsic meaning. I could probably do it with chicken bones. They are a point of focus and concentration for me and for the client.

I usually don't look more than six months ahead.

Give two good examples of your telepathy. Once I got an image of a plump woman in a blue dress. She was smiling and happy, but I could only see her from the waist up. I found out later that she was in a wheelchair after being injured in an automobile accident.

On another occasion, when I was reading for a young woman, I told her she was in love with a married man who had two children. She heatedly denied the fact. But I described him to her. She later called me with her apologies. The man she was seeing never told her he was married, with two children.

What was your most uncomfortably accurate prediction? When I was reading for a woman whose boyfriend worked for the CIA, I elaborated on many of its activities. The woman recorded the reading and played the tape for him. He was startled at its accuracy and wanted her to destroy the tape to protect his private missions. She talked him out of it.

Have you ever known something the person would rather you didn't know? Someone once brought a friend to me who was a professional football player. Although he walked perfectly, I saw that he had a bad knee and asked him about it. He wasn't impressed because it had been in the papers, even though I don't read the sports pages and didn't know in advance I'd see him.

But then I said to him, "You're also having trouble with your other knee." He was really shocked—and upset—because he hadn't told anyone since he didn't want to jeopardize his contract negotiations.

How did you become involved in psychic phenomena? In the mid-'60s, a friend and I went to a Gypsy tea kettle place for tea leaf readings. The sweet little old lady told me a long story about a man I would meet: He would be dark, like boats and motorcycles, and I would marry him.

It hit me afterward that the reading had to do with a *friend* in Florida, not me. I wrote the friend, and she married the man. After this experience, I said to myself, "I can do this," and began studying the process. I bought cards because I am not crazy about tea.

Have you ever seen a spirit or apparition? Yes, usually connected with people I am reading for. They appear like smoke. I describe them to the people, and they turn out to be their relatives who have departed.

Cite a specific incident. I had one terrifying experience with one. I was meditating in a pitch-black room and heard a deep, raspy male voice gasping behind me. I wondered if someone had broken into the house, although I knew no one had. I turned on every light, but no one was there. It took an hour for the sound to subside.

Have you ever experimented with Ouija or séances? Yes, but I am more cautious and will not do it anymore.

Why? The scenes were like something out of a horror movie. There were raps and taps, and the table would lift up and bang down. There were knocks on the wood like Ping-Pong balls. It often felt like something was shooting inside the table. Heavy chairs that normally took two men to lift rose easily.

Once, when a cynic was among us, the long, heavy wooden table jammed into his chest. He left and did not return.

Is there a spiritual reason that you don't like Ouija boards? The more I read, the more I realized that I could tap into something undesirable. I don't want to conjure up two-o'clock-in-the-morning movies, but there are elements we are not aware of, including divine elements that should be left alone.

I don't have all the answers about this, but I'm aware that some things beyond our dimension could possibly be harmful. I feel that my work is a gift that is connected to a higher ability.

Professora
Selegna

C/O 444 BRICKELL AVENUE, SUITE 900
MIAMI, FLORIDA 33131

*The most famous Hispanic psychic in
the world, she is seen by millions on
Spanish-language TV shows and
infomercials in America.*

Do you have any spirit guides? Yes, a woman I call
"the blue lady," who does not believe in astrology, and a
gentleman, who does believe. I have heard them talking, and
she says, "I don't like your little numbers." And he says,
"But my little numbers are the ones that tell the truth."
Even though they don't agree, they usually come to the same
conclusions about what is going to happen to someone!

When did you first see them? I've been hearing and
seeing them since I was three, but I didn't know they were

spirits. I thought everybody else could see them, too. To me they were normal.

Was your family supportive of this? No. One day, a Good Friday, I was talking to the lady, and my grandmother caught me. She took me to a woman who hit me on my legs so hard with leaves they left marks. I guess this woman who beat me was trying to take away my spirits.

Did she? I didn't see my spirits again until I was seventeen. Then, one night, I was ready to go to sleep, and I saw the lady again: She was not one day older. I got excited, but she put her finger over her mouth for me to be quiet. And she said, "Don't ever tell your family that you see me because I don't want for them to take me away from you again." And soon after that, the man came back, and then they started coming back together.

What cases are you happiest to have been involved with? About nine years ago, a client of mine with a teenage daughter called me at about eleven o'clock at night. Her daughter was supposed to be home at seven that night, but she hadn't come back. I looked at the girl's chart, and immediately I got a bad psychic feeling.

What did you see? A house with a lot of children behind a door, and one of them was her daughter. Then the man (my male spirit guide) appeared and showed me a little telephone book and an address underlined in red. I called my client back and told her, "Look in your daughter's telephone book for an address underlined in red. Then call the police and give them that number."

Did she go along with what you suggested? At first, she said she couldn't do anything because she had called the police and they wouldn't look for her daughter until she'd been gone twenty-four hours.

But I told her, "Then you find out where that number is and go over, because when I look at her chart, I see you don't have much time to save this girl. And if you do not rescue her before six o'clock tomorrow morning, some people are going to take her to another country."

She went to the place with the underlined red number that night, and she called me the next day and said her daughter was found there with a bunch of guys that traffic girls for prostitution. They were planning to take her to another country that day. And her mother saved her.

How did you become so successful? It wasn't easy. I was born and educated as an accountant in Cuba. But I never practiced. I came here and did readings.

Then I started getting into television and radio, and in 1987, I got my own television show from eight to nine every night in Miami. And then I did predictions for a very big Univision show.

Now I appear on the largest worldwide Spanish-language psychic infomercial program—it's called *Alianza Espiritual*—and it's seen in many cities in America like Miami and Los Angeles.

Do you consider yourself to be more a psychic or an astrologer? Both. I was born a psychic, but I was trained as an astrologer. When I'm reading a chart, many times I see a lot of things that are not in the chart of the person.

Why do you think you have become so popular on television? I will not lie. I will tell you like it is. I think people get my vibration and know I have a lot of credibility. I do not act. I am myself. When I talk to people, they think I am in their living room.

MONNICA SEPULVEDA

2064 SEASCAPE BOULEVARD
APTOS, CALIFORNIA 95003
(408) 688-8884

Amber Christopher

*She calls herself a solution-oriented
psychic therapist, and she uses
neurolinguistics and obtains help
from the angel Gabrielle.*

***How did you realize you were different from
other children?*** I have always been sensitive. As a child
I thought everyone had these feelings. But I was really more
empathetic, actually feeling what other people were feeling.

What was your first paranormal experience? It
occurred when I was twelve. I had undergone surgery on
my eyes a few years before, and I was wearing glasses, which
were blue-and-white checked and very ugly. An angel came
to me and gave me a statement to repeat once daily for a
year. "I see through the eyes of God, for God is within me,

and we are one. God's vision is perfect, and my vision is perfect. And for this I give thanks today." I repeated it, and at thirteen I had normal vision and threw my glasses away.

How do angels help you now? Two years ago, I flew from L.A. to New York to do *The Maury Povich Show*. I had been delayed in Denver en route and was very stressed. It was around two in the morning in New York, and I was afraid to go to sleep for fear my body clock would maintain Pacific Time and I wouldn't wake up in time for the show. But I also wanted to make sure I would have plenty of energy.

Did an angel appear on the airplane? Yes, that was the first time the angel Gabrielle appeared to me. She assured me that all would be OK. In the end, I got no sleep but did well on the program.

Who is Gabrielle? She's not the male archangel Gabriel. Gabrielle, who has been helping me since she appeared to me in the plane, is huge and beautiful and has wings.

Describe your work in the field of life after death. In the twenty-three years that I've been counseling people psychically, I particularly like when a person's deceased family member appears during a reading. That to me is proof of life after death.

Relate an episode in which one appeared. One time a woman's father appeared in the middle of her reading. He was standing as if posing for a photo, with a golf trophy and a club and a golf buddy. He said, "All I do is play golf," and he named the friends he played with. The woman told me that throughout his lifetime, he always said he would spend eternity playing golf with those same golf buddies.

Any others you like? Well, another time I was counseling a woman whose husband had passed away two or three months before. The husband had heard me on the radio and always planned to see me for a reading, but he was killed in a motorcycle accident. While I was doing a reading for her, I saw her husband coming up behind her with a rose, and then he gave her a kiss.

How did she react when you told her that? She cried because she told me that that's what her husband did every Friday; he came up from behind her and handed her a rose. And when she told me that, *I* cried, too. In that reading, her husband also gave her pertinent information regarding insurance and papers he'd left behind.

Do you get involved with haunted houses? Frankly, it gives me the heebie-jeebies to see spirits, but it's worth it because it brings people peace of mind. But when houses have disturbances, I tune in and find out who it is who's bothering the owner, why the spirits are there, and help them let go so they can move on to the next level since they're stuck.

How would you describe your practice? Solution oriented. The idea is not for people to stay in the problem but to go to the *solution*, change gears, and turn around. To just predict "this is the way it is going to be" would make me a doomsday prophet. Then there would be no free will.

What is the purpose of your readings? To help people help themselves. People today are too stressed. They need to be more independent. To connect to the higher powers within themselves. It is not up to me to do that for them because all the answers are contained within. It's just my job to get the message out.

Do you do that with a book or tape? Yes, I wrote and sell a tape package whose purpose is to put me out of business! The *Internal Equalizer* is designed to make people less dependent on psychics. I thought too many of my clients were coming to see me too many times. They wanted me to make their decisions for them and give them a quick fix. I think psychics should help people find the answers within themselves.

Do psychics need psychics, too? Absolutely. Linda Georgian* and I are really good friends, and we pick up on each other whenever we talk. When two psychics get together, we can't help it. Inevitably we start reading for each other without even trying.

---

*See page 289.

*See page 289.

SHIRLEE TEABO

226 SOUTH 312TH STREET
FEDERAL WAY, WASHINGTON 98003
FAX: (206) 941-4895
E-MAIL: Teabo@escape.com

Matryx Photography

*She calls herself a megapsychic, once
lived in a haunted house, and has
worked to communicate telepathically
with a dolphin.*

How would you describe yourself? I'm not a
stranger who, with the turn of a card, changes lives. I believe
people must stay in control of their own destiny. I read tarot
cards for people one-on-one, in person, or over the phone.
They're just a point of concentration. I could use a crystal
ball or goat innards, but tarot cards are lighter than a ball
and less messy than the goat innards!

Who are your clients? One third of my customers are
men. Businesspeople seek my advice on new product development, personnel changes, marketplace trends, where to

locate new facilities, and the best time to take action on certain things.

What other psychic areas have you gotten into? I've also been called in by investigators on various Pacific Northwest homicides, including the Ted Bundy case. Two law enforcement officers drove me around a heavily wooded area where some of the victim's remains had been found. They told me, "Any time you feel anything say, 'Stop.'"

Did you find anything? Yes. I did find some material relating to the Bundy victims. There were also spots where I felt uncomfortable that something else had happened. And when they went back and checked, we learned that some of those places were where other crimes of violence had taken place, one even fifty years earlier.

Did you do something interesting before you became a psychic? Although I grew up in a regular upper-middle-class family in Washington, I spent almost four years in the navy; I did just about everything from mopping floors to military intelligence, depending on what trouble I was in that week. I did a lot of floors. Still, I loved the navy, contrary to my free spirit women's lib attitude.

How did you get into the psychic area full-time? At the beginning of 1966, I was blind for a few weeks when I burned my eyes with hair coloring. My sight returned, but when you lose one sense, others develop. That's when my psychic abilities became sharper.

Did any personal events contribute to this also? My husband and I had adopted a baby, and then we adopted twins—that was our second litter—thirteen months after our first. My husband started a successful software company, and we went from a half million dollars in personal assets to owing two hundred fifty thousand dollars in back taxes in less than a year. He went to Europe to try to raise money and stayed there three years instead of three weeks.

What happened then? While he was there, someone bought me a deck of tarot cards. My father had just been killed in a train accident. My mother had no money. I was living on welfare in a house that was haunted with my mother, three kids, and a deck of cards I couldn't read.

The first time I read for someone I charged the person five dollars an hour. I felt like a hooker. If someone had told me twenty-five years ago that this is what I'd be doing for a living I'd say, "You're out of your mind." I thought psychics were fat people wearing turbans.

But everything I have now I've earned through that deck of cards. I've raised my kids, and I supported my mother for nineteen years until she passed away.

You mentioned a haunted house. What was the story there? I moved into a house when I got married. The first night I heard crying. By the third night, we put axes under the bed to protect ourselves.

One day my husband blamed the cats for a shredded tie. Soon after he left for work, utter chaos took place. Wedding gifts were broken, and his ties were tied into knots and thrown into the wastebasket. Afterward, he thought I had created this disaster.

Did anyone else see these things? One night, we had a state senator and his wife over for dinner. A plate on the wall flew across the room. The chandelier started swinging. The couple left and never hung out with us again. Fortunately for me, when psychic things have happened, there have been others around me so I wasn't put away in a rubber room!

How did you find the ghosts? One day neighbors came to my house with a Ouija board. I was the reluctant virgin. When I said I didn't believe in Ouija boards, one of the curtains burst into flames! I asked the board if a ghost was hanging around. It spelled out, "My house. Help my boy." That scared the hell out of me. I've never touched a Ouija board since.

What about the ghost in the house? Oh, yes. When I traced the history of the house, I learned it was owned by a couple who had an adopted child nicknamed TNT because of his wild behavior. They were killed in an automobile accident so we were dealing with people who didn't know they were dead.

For three nights my husband and I kept saying, "You're dead. Go in peace." They went, but we gave the house to my mother and moved out because of the haunting. Then, as I said, I came back to that house years later.

Give an example of some accurate warning you've given a client. I told a woman who had a yellow Volkswagen to be real careful the first week of December because I saw her having an accident. She said, "That's a piece of cake. It's my vacation time so I'll stay home." She took care of her grandson, who had a little toy Volkswagen on the kitchen floor, and she stepped on it and broke her leg.

How did your dolphin telepathy attempts go? I tried to prove that a dolphin in British Columbia named Whitewing was telepathic. I traveled 160 miles each time to see her. I was told that as soon as I hit the Canadian border, she'd start dancing in the pool.

Also, we would mentally throw a ball to each other, and I just knew when she was catching it. She did a better job than I did! We were trying to send things telepathically back and forth, but she's audio and I'm visual. I feel she was very telepathic; I was a dud.

What kind of psychics should people look for? Look for psychics with a permanent address, who don't have trappings like beads in their doorways or spooky music.

What are some of your ideas about your unique occupation? I don't think any good psychics know how they're doing it. Being an excellent psychic takes discipline, but as long as you don't believe your own press, you can do good work with people.

My first loyalty is to the person who pays the wages.

I can only predict positive events for people because I'm a positive person.

I used to ask about my psychic abilities: "Why me?" Now I ask, "Why not me?"

I write a newspaper column on parapsychology, and I tell people that parapsychology is yesterday's suspicion, today's science, and tomorrow's answers.

Wendy! The Psychics' Psychic®

POST OFFICE BOX 490, GRACIE STATION
NEW YORK, NEW YORK 10028
(212) 734-9002
FAX: (212) 439-9109

She's president of the Professional Psychics of America and has a cable TV show in New York.

How can people tell if they have a good psychic? Some will ask you questions instead of giving you information, and then they'll feed you back what you told them. You might as well have given yourself a reading!

What's a trick used by bad psychics? I call one twenty questions. You have to be careful of this when calling in advance for an appointment. You'll forget a month after you called that in your first conversation you mentioned something to the psychic about your lost job, your child's problems at school, or whatever. Then during the reading, they feed this information back to you, and you don't remember that they got it from *you* earlier!

As a watchdog for psychics, what else do you want to warn people about? They should also watch out for psychics who are too vague or hypothetical. The two most popular words of the psychic wanna-be are *if* and *maybe*.

In our industry, there is no license or certification, so anyone can go into business, hurting the credibility of the professional. It can also hurt their clients, because psychics have as much influence on their clients as psychologists or other helping professionals. There are a great number of quacks in our industry who mislead and frighten people.

You call yourself the psychics' psychic. Why do other psychics come to you? Although I believe that everyone is born with intuition, everyone can't be a great psychic any more than every musician or tennis player can be an Isaac Stern or a Martina Navratilova. Other psychics come to me because they have confidence in my abilities.

Why? I don't solicit information from clients, and I discourage them from telling me facts about themselves. I also don't interrogate people to look for information that *I'm* supposed to tell them.

I feel that I am a provider of information, like a road map. I make it easier for people to navigate by giving them all the right details.

How do you work? I have trained myself to turn my abilities on and off. Otherwise, I would be open to all kinds of energies, including negative ones.

I have many phone clients I've never met, but I can tell many things about them, for example, I can pick up what they look like. I'll tell them things like, "You cut your hair so short," or "I love your blond highlights." I might also mention that their apartment is a mess with all that laundry piled up!

How long have you been a psychic? I have always been psychic and thought that was normal, even within my conservative family upbringing. When I was a child, I frequently knew who was calling on the phone or what was in the mail. I used to locate missing objects for my mother.

What is your technique? Before people arrive for a reading, I focus on their physical description: health, career, emotional state, and things like that. I often receive images of family members and other people in the individual's life. I write this down and show it to them when they come. My clients often tell me that I answer their questions before they ask them.

Describe the work you've done as a medium. I often pick up how someone died. I actually feel the death. If someone had a stroke, I'll feel my head explode. If it's a heart attack, I'll get a pain in my chest. The deceased often give valuable information such as details necessary for the will.

Can you tell about a reading in this area? One time, I was reading to a man whose wife has passed on. She came through to tell her husband, "Please stop eating all those bagels with your coffee. You'll stuff up your system and constipate yourself." He responded, "She's still nagging me about that from the other side!"

Describe something unique that you do in the psychic area. I assist people in their residential needs. If someone wants to buy a house, I can tell them everything that is wrong with it: if the pipes or roof leak, if the foundation is shaky, or if a new addition has been put on.

In an apartment situation, I can tell them what the building is like, what kind of people live there, whether it is noisy or quiet, and what the landlord is like.

What other areas do you work in? I do stock market predictions for international clients. I am the only psychic that I know of who accurately predicted the stock market crash of 1987 to the exact week. I had sent out a press release months before to many financial editors and clients, and there was an article about my accurate prediction in *Forbes* magazine and the *National Enquirer*.

Did you ever do anything professionally besides psychic work? I was a very successful photographer. I exhibited in Europe, France, and Spain and have been featured in some of Europe's most prestigious photograph magazines. I once photographed Princess Grace.

Have you used your talents to help yourself? My psychic ability has saved my life several times. For example, on December 31, 1986, a friend and I were in Puerto Rico. We were walking to the Dupont Plaza Hotel to check out New Year's Eve accommodations and to do a little gambling. I had a terrible feeling and refused to go into the hotel. One-half hour later, people at the Dupont were screaming and jumping out of windows. That was the biggest hotel fire in Puerto Rican history, and there were a staggering number of deaths.

STACEY ANNE WOLF

POST OFFICE BOX 3483
GRAND CENTRAL STATION
NEW YORK, NY 10163
(212) 330-8189
E-MAIL: SWPSYCHIC@aol.com

Glenn Jussen/The Jussen Studio

America's youngest successful psychic, she's been dubbed the Generation X psychic and the "sexy psychic," and she's also a stand-up comedian and actress.

What's the hardest thing to get used to as a psychic? I have a lot of one-sided conversations with people. I'll see a client and say, "You're getting your hair done tomorrow," or "Your daughter is going to be in the school play." People don't even have to talk back to me. I just *know.*

What are some of the psychic jokes in your stand-up comedy routine? I pick out a guy in the audience and ask, "Do you believe in past lives, sir?" And he'll usually say no. And I'll say, "Well, I see that in your past you could have been my brother. No, wait, maybe it was my sister. I want my dress back. And Mom wants to know why you haven't called her in two hundred years."

Or I tell the audience, "I'm such a good psychic I write my diary a week in advance."

Or someone from the audience will shout, "If you're really psychic, what's my name?" And I say, "Let me guess. 'Loser'? Do you really want me to guess your name—or what everyone else calls you?"

And sometimes when I start by saying to the audience, "I'm psychic," if there's no reaction, I say, "You don't care? I knew that."

How did being a psychic help you when you were younger? When I got older, I always knew exactly what was going to happen throughout the day so I knew what I needed to carry with me. Band-Aids. Nail files. I had it all. My friends were amazed. "You always have everything," they'd say to me. "No," I'd say, "I only have what I need."

Do your clients like the fact that you're so young? I'm guess I've got a Generation X attitude. My older clients find my young energy refreshing and are able to see the changes occurring in America through my eyes.

Were you successful in your career before this? I was an actress, and people may have seen me if they've taken a Continental Airlines flight. I'm the one doing the safety video they show at takeoff! Before I did that job, I went to work at MTV, but my show was canceled.

What led you to become a professional psychic? After my show was canceled and I was unemployed, I had time on my hands. I went to a tarot reader who was really bad, and I thought, *I can do better than that.* With plenty of free time and nothing to do, I studied my new private passion—the tarot cards. That was my spiritual awakening.

Why do some people dislike tarot card readings? People think the cards are doing things, but it's not true. They're just a laminated deck of cardboard. The *universe* is putting them into order.

There are seventy-eight cards, each with its own distinct

picture and meaning. They're used to forecast probable future outcomes and clarify unresolved issues. People shouldn't fear the cards because they have no power over them. All of us can get whatever we want. It's just a matter of time.

Are all tarot card readers doing pretty much the same thing? No, for one thing, we're different as people. An old term for tarot readers is fortune-tellers, but it's a myth that all tarot readers must be Gypsies. They come from a variety of backgrounds and are everyday people, like myself.

All readers develop their own way of reading the cards and their own unique way of answering the questions posed to them by the client. So if you don't like something about the reading, you can simply choose not to believe it. Tarot card readers are not infallible. It is impossible to have every answer to every question.

You were described on one TV show as a sports psychic. Do you know much about sports? Nothing. It's a real test for me to do that kind of work because I'm either right or wrong. I must generally be right because I have a professional sports enthusiast who calls me five times a week even though I know nothing about sports.

How do you do it? I just need the name of the teams, college or professional—most of them I've never heard of— and then I choose the team that will win. I also pick the point spread. It's not something I do more than twenty minutes a day and I'm very accurate. I like testing my abilities.

You also do past-life counseling. How can someone's past life help them today? One lawyer that I read for had a reoccurring past-life dream, and I correctly described it to him. It was a Civil War battle, he was leading it, and his boldness got him killed.

How did that help him? In this life, he's very timid and accepts the opinion of everyone over his and puts himself behind the pack. I showed him that his boldness and courage may have worked against him in his past life, but in this one I saw that it would enhance him. He listened to me, and now he's doing much better in business.

How do you help your clients in this life? I had a few clients who weren't happy here in New York but were afraid of moving. I told one client, who was not comfortable in her skin, that she would be happier if she would make some changes. I thought she should wear more blue and purple clothing, change her name, allow her source to come out more, and move down south. She took my advice and is much happier.

How accurate are you? Many people tell me that whatever I say to them comes true. They'll lose their job, and I tell them that they're going to get an offer for a better job with more money in six weeks that is more managerial—and it happens.

MORE GENERAL PSYCHICS

LAURIE A. BAUM,
M.S.W., C.S.W.

61 WEST 62ND STREET, SUITE 4G
NEW YORK, NEW YORK 10023
(212) 606-3782

VICTORIA BEARDEN

POST OFFICE BOX 1415
SOLANA BEACH, CALIFORNIA 92075
(800) 771-4266

CHAR

MICHIGAN
(810) 356-5360

B. Ann Gehman

7317 WESTMORE DRIVE
SPRINGFIELD, VIRGINIA 22150
(703) 451-7705

Peggy Hensley

POST OFFICE BOX 1025
RICHMOND, INDIANA 47375
(317) 962-0296

Jojo Savard

444 BRICKELL AVENUE, SUITE 900
MIAMI, FLORIDA 33131
(The most famous psychic in Canada, she also works
in the United States.)

Jim Watson

METAPHYSICAL–ESP CENTER
8240 BEVERLY BOULEVARD, SUITE 3
LOS ANGELES, CALIFORIA 90048
(213) 852-1550
FAX: (213) 651-3773

CHAPTER
10

The Five Most Famous Psychics in America

DOROTHY ALLISON

BOX 205
NUTLEY, NEW JERSEY 07110

Alexander M. Allison, Photographer

Often called the "psychic sleuth," for decades she's been the best-known psychic crime detective in the country.

How do you begin an investigation for a missing person? When possible, I start by being in close contact with their relatives. I hold their hands, I get impressions from them, I talk with them—but not about the case. I don't discuss that with anyone, and I don't read anything about it. I like to go to each scene cold, without any preparation or information.

How do you find a body for the police? I don't have to be near the person to find him or her. I can be thousands of miles away and still get clues. Sometimes I draw a map for the police of where they will find the body they're looking for—although I get lost whenever I try to use a map to get somewhere myself!

If you're not there, how can you tell the police exactly where to look if, say, the body is in the woods? If the body is where there's no one around, just woods, I'll show them the area *outside* and say, "Mr. Jones lives here," or "Mr. Smith there." And then I put them in direct line with the body. Or I will get the name of a street and say, "If you come out of the wooded area where the body is, you will find this street or this house."

Do cases have to be fresh for you to solve them? Time is irrelevant for me. A little girl in Colorado was missing in 1991, and the authorities contacted me in 1992. I told them the name of the man who murdered her. It was a common name, spelled differently because of one letter, and I spelled it 100 percent correctly. Her body was found in 1993, and they caught the accused killer in 1995 in another state.

What did you learn later about the case? The killer lived a half a mile away at the time. I think the mother had taken the victim's little sister or brother to go to a church meeting. The killer saw the mother leave the house, and he went into the bedroom, took the little girl out, and murdered her.

Where does your information come from? I don't know. I've been psychic since I was a child, but clairvoyance, telepathy, and extrasensory perception aren't words I use to describe what I do because I don't know anything about those. It's just natural for me to see a kaleidoscope of pictures in my mind.

Are you better at some times than others? I don't see these visions if I'm tired or distracted. Also, I've got to be able to tune everybody and everything out and concentrate only on what I am doing. I have to filter out anything extraneous so that my psychic abilities won't be drained or diverted.

When does your information come to you? During dreams or when I'm awake, just having a cup of coffee or whatever. They may be of events in the past or the future or a thought transmitted by someone in the room. I often don't know the significance of it myself until the case is over.

What was your first major case? The first time I helped the police was in 1968. In a dream I saw a blond, blue-eyed boy in a green snowsuit drowned in a pond and stuck in a drainpipe. Oddly, his shoes were on the wrong feet.

A year later, a missing blond-haired, blue-eyed child was found in a green snowsuit stuck in a drainpipe in a pond just as I described—and his shoes were on the wrong feet! By the way, the family could not afford a funeral so I covered the expenses.

Drownings are still what I do best—maybe because this first case was a drowning!

Describe a typical case you've worked on. A twenty-three-year-old woman named Glenda Harter was seen drinking in a bar alone. She left the place alone as well. A few months later, a torso and a hand with no fingertips left on it was found, but no one knew if it was hers.

When the police called me, I told them that the number seventeen would play a role in the case, that the suspect lived in a reddish-colored house located near the fire station.

Were you correct? When the detectives went to talk to someone they suspected was the killer, it was May 17. He lived in a reddish house. And it was located two blocks from the fire station. When he was asked about the woman who disappeared, he immediately confessed to the murder.

Describe a case involving children. I helped locate the bodies of two infants who had been killed by their mentally ill mother. She told the police that she threw her two children off a bridge so they wouldn't become sinners. But she didn't say which bridge it was. The police looked for the children but couldn't find them.

What did you tell them? I saw the numbers seven and eight and told the police to look where they saw doubles. Then, at the base of a railroad bridge, they found the number seventy-eight, in the river was a buoy with the number forty-four, and in a nearby parking lot was a pair of identical electrical transformers. The decomposed bodies of the two children were found nearby.

How accurate were you in the Patty Hearst case?
I was the first psychic called by Randolph Hearst after his daughter Patty was kidnapped. I foresaw that she would be brainwashed by her kidnappers and become involved with them. I warned the FBI that Patty was at first held in a closet-type cell against her will. When everyone in the country, including every FBI agent, was looking for her, I told the FBI at one point that she was in Pennsylvania. That turned out to be true, although it didn't come out until long after she was caught.

Did you make any predictions concerning her capture? Yes, I told the media she would be found alive and unhurt. And I foresaw a blazing holocaust, and a fire ultimately killed Symbionese Liberation Army leader Donald De Freeze and five of his gang.

How do you feel about the criminals you've helped apprehend? I'd like to see all killers convicted, especially those who rape their victims. I have seen some horrible things. One can never forget the scenes of some crimes, especially those that contain the bodies of little children.

How many cases have you worked on? I have helped on more than four thousand cases with dozens of police departments from all around the country over the past twenty-seven years. Besides the Patty Hearst case, my famous ones include the Son of Sam murders, the Atlanta child murders, and the John Wayne Gacy case.

GEORGE ANDERSON, JR.

C/O INTERNATIONAL ARTISTS GROUP
1993 DEER PARK AVENUE
DEER PARK, NEW YORK 11729
(516) 243-4600
FAX: (516) 243-4907

Hugo LaMonica

*For his ability to talk to those who have
passed over, he has become one of the
most famous psychics in America.*

**What is the difference between personal contact
with loved ones and receiving regular messages
from someone else?** I don't know enough about channeling to really have an opinion on it. I can only talk about
myself and mediumship. But I find it easier and more appeal-
ing to deal with your great-grandfather or your favorite
cousin than with somebody who died in the arena with Spar-
tacus.

What are the most touching cases for you? Those
involving parents losing children, especially, those who have
lost them through miscarriages, SIDS, stillbirths, or abor-

tions. Society gives these people very little support, and it can also be frustrating for children who have passed over to see their bereaved parents feeling abandoned.

What do you tell these parents? I often have to relay to them from their offspring that it was simply "my time to go." Bereaved parents often say to me afterward, "I feel better knowing my child is not alone. Now I know I can talk to my child whenever I want to. It is a great comfort to know that they will not forget me and that we will all be together soon."

Do some of the departed send you stronger messages than others? There seems to be a connection between tragic, unusual, or very emotional circumstances at passing and the strength and clarity of the spirit's communication.

Someone whose passing left loved ones with regret or severe grief seems to make an extra effort to provide solace. In contrast, when we look at a grandparent who quietly passed away at a ripe old age of natural causes, they usually have little to say.

Can you give an example of a case in which someone had an emotional passing and there was a strong communication afterward with the family? A ten-year-old boy named Charles was killed by three other kids slightly older than he was. They approached Charles and demanded he hand over his denim jacket. When he refused, they attacked him and stuffed several cotton bandannas down his throat. He choked to death.

What happened then? The three boys were accused of the murder. The father of one of them requested my help. Through me, Charles sent forgiving vibrations for this man's son, which comforted and relieved the father.

When did you reveal to the world that you could communicate with the departed? After I graduated from high school and college and got a job for the telephone company, I began doing readings on a local radio show. It was 1980, and I explained to the audience that I could communicate with the hereafter. The departed spoke to me or sent pictures, and I then deciphered their meaning. After only a few appearances on the radio, I became quite popular. By 1981, I was cohosting my own show.

Did you start life off "normally"? Absolutely. I was born on August 17, 1952, in Long Island. My father worked for the Pennsylvania Railroad, and my mother was a housewife. Everyone called me Baby George because I was the youngest of three children. I had a totally normal early childhood.

What happened then? When I was six years old, I got chicken pox. Complications set in, and a virus attacked my central nervous system. I got encephalitis and was paralyzed for two months.

I was never the same after I recovered. Suddenly, I could tell people what had happened to them and what had happened to those around them in the past—sometimes before I was born.

When did you start sharing your visions with others? Around the same time, I began to be able to see spirits of deceased people. I thought there was nothing unusual about it, and I even told my friend Tommy that his grandmother had black around her and would soon be going over to the other side. His negative reaction to this confused me and caused me to be more careful about telling people these things in the future. I began revealing my information only to those I felt believed me.

Did you have any spirit companions? Yes. For example, one, the Lilac Lady, as I called her, was a woman in lilac robes who appeared whenever I was a little down. In school, I occasionally spoke of these spirits and my visions, and the nuns began worrying and keeping an eye on me. My fellow classmates taunted me.

Do you remember any specific incidents? One day, a bully was trying to stuff me into a locker. I said, "I see that your father is a drunk and beats up on you and your mother every night." After that, the students became afraid of me and shied away. I became a loner.

Did your visions lead others to misunderstand you? As the visions became stronger, I confided about them to a nun. She told my parents. The school authorities thought I was about to have a nervous breakdown, and they even sent me to a mental health center for testing. And then, a psychiatrist wrongly diagnosed me as a passive schizophrenic!

What type of state are you in during your readings? Experts have monitored my physical responses with an electrocardiograph to measure my heart rate and an electroencephalograph to measure my brain wave activity.

My brain waves alternate between alpha, a state of deep relaxation and passive awareness, to beta, an alert, physically active state. My heart rate increases from the normal 70 beats per minute to 113 or 114 during a trance state.

LINDA GEORGIAN

1565 WYN COVE DRIVE
VERO BEACH, FLORIDA 32963
(407) 231-9977
FAX: (407) 231-4007

Tiffany Studio

A former physical education and health teacher, she is now the most often seen psychic in America.

How do you feel about those who disapprove of your being involved in a psychic hot line? I know there are those who criticize telephone psychic lines, but God would never allow me to be involved with anything that didn't help people or was a scam.

How would you describe yourself? I am totally sincere. I take my work extremely seriously. I'm not on TV making predictions and not knowing what I'm doing. Although I'm very religious, I don't foist my beliefs on others. Because I work with guardian angels doesn't mean you have to believe in them. If you don't, change the channel and watch something else.

What don't you like about some psychics? I don't like people who light candles and try to bring others back from the dead. My psychic powers come from within my soul, not a twenty-five-thousand-year-old entity or a crystal or some other object.

What do your own powers include? Clairvoyance, clairaudience, automatic writing, mental telepathy, Kirlian photography, healing, occasional astral travel, plus aura reading. Everyone has an aura. I began seeing auras around people when I was twelve. People meet somebody for the first time and say, "There's something about this person I don't like." Well, they're picking up on the person's aura.

Does your psychic ability extend to yourself? My own psychic ability told me I was going to be a success, so I was obviously right there. But I don't claim to be 100 percent accurate for myself all the time—or for others. I don't feel that I know all or see all.

In 1973 I predicted that at this time in my life I'd be married with three children. I'm single with a dog. Now I don't see a marriage in my future, but maybe I'll be wrong there, too.

What trends do you see in the psychic realm? I'm seeing more men becoming interested in this. In the last few years, many of the calls I've gotten on radio and TV are coming from men, often calling from cellular phones in their cars.

People are also more willing to talk about their guardian angels now. Angels appear in all religions. Most of the population believes in them, but until recently, they kept their beliefs private. Now it's very open. In fact, I just wrote a book about it called *Your Guardian Angels.*

What is your background? I was born in Cleveland, Ohio, of Italian ancestry. I was a compulsive straight-A student and overachiever plus an award-winning drum majorette who would cry in the bathroom if I got a B.

Although I saw auras when I was young, I didn't start "reading" people until I was older. But in college, my roommates would come to me for advice, asking me whether they would get an A or a B on an exam or hear from a boyfriend at a certain time. Because I was close to God, having grown up in a strict Catholic environment, I felt this had a lot to do with my burgeoning psychic abilities.

What did you do professionally before becoming a full-time professional psychic? I have a master's in learning disabilities from the Florida Institute of Technology. I have also studied divinity, naturopathy, and herbology. In the '70s I was a gym teacher in a high school in Florida, refereeing basketball games. Then I was a health coordinator for a school system, but they weren't interested in health and nutrition—just giving children candy and fast food.

When did you start traveling the psychic road? After college, in 1968, I decided to go to Japan to study meditation and Eastern religion for a year. I chose Japan because I believed in reincarnation and thought that I had lived at least one previous lifetime in Japan. I wanted to find my roots there.

Did you go with anyone else? I went alone because I wanted to force myself to talk to the spirits. I thought if I went to a completely foreign land where I didn't know the language of the people, it would force me to depend on the guidance of God, Jesus, and the angels for every move I made.

Did your life change while you were there? God spoke to me for the first time. I was told that my assignment was to help as many people as possible. If I worked hard at it, He would provide the people and opportunities I needed. Now I feel I'm right next to God, interpreting. It's my life's mission.

Did you do other shows before Psychic Friends Network (PFN)? Fame didn't just happen. I've worked hard. Before the Psychic Friends Network, I did a psychic-oriented talk radio program in Hawaii. And while I was working as a physical education teacher, I began producing a cable television show in Fort Lauderdale on the side. I spent about fifty thousand dollars of my own money promoting that show throughout Florida, and it lasted for ten years.

What do you have to do with your show today? Not only am I on it, but PFN uses a network of sixteen hundred psychics, and I'm involved in the quality control of them.

Who are your guardian angels? I assign angels to everything in my life, and I keep updating the list. For example, I have a diet angel, who keeps me eating the right foods; an exercise angel, who encourages me to exercise; a headache angel, who is probably one of my most important ones since he keeps me from having headaches; a safety and protection angel; a financial angel; a business opportunity angel, who is like an angelic networker; a fun and laughter angel, who makes sure I have enough of both; and others as well.

What are guardian angels like? They can be either sex and they appear, disappear, and reappear. They can become visible when you want them to and can appear in any form we want. There is no limit to the number of angels who will come to our aid.

They stay with us even after death, guiding us, going over the lessons we've learned, and assisting our souls as we prepare to move on. They can help you from day to day if you stay in close contact with them. If you want to help yourself, call upon these angels to guide and lead you.

What do you do for your personal clients? I can read a person's aura not only face-to-face but over the telephone, telepathically, just as I can read minds without being in the same room as the person I'm reading.

People want to hear that I have some magical powers, that I can change their lives, but I can't. I don't know all or see all. Nobody does. I tell people how to catch the pot at the end of the rainbow. That's what I'm all about.

What specifically do you teach them? I help them learn how to practice positive thinking and imagery so they can attain the things they want. I suggest to people that they make "destiny scrapbooks" so they can see positive images of what they want to achieve. I tell them to cut out pictures of things they want in order to help the images become embedded in the subconscious. The more people program and actually feel the reality of it, the more they'll feel like they actually have it.

Besides helping people see their futures and make plans, I also treat my clients holistically. Americans don't pay enough attention to diet, exercise, and the mind. They just want pills.

Have you achieved your goals? Others might think so. I am the most televised psychic in the world. Since 1992, I am seen an average of 280 times a week with Dionne Warwicke on the most successful syndicated psychic infomercial ever: "The Psychic Friends Network." I'm financially successful, which is how it should be, because God does not expect me or anyone else to be poor.

Is there anything else you would want? I still want more—not money but a chance to reach out and help even more people. My goal now is for my new national psychic and holistic television talk show to be successful. And I wouldn't mind running a TV network focused on the metaphysical for people who want to hear about spiritual matters but don't feel comfortable with *The 700 Club.*

IRENE HUGHES

500 NORTH MICHIGAN AVENUE, SUITE 1040
CHICAGO, ILLINOIS 60611
(312) 467-1140

William J. Frantz

World famous for over twenty-five years, she predicted the assassinations of Robert and Jack Kennedy, Chappaquiddick, and many other world events.

After more than twenty years as one of the world's most successful psychics, do you ever worry about competition? Twenty years ago I was listed as one of the top ten psychics in America by *Pageant* magazine. A few years ago I was listed as one of the world's ten most amazing psychics by the *National Enquirer*. I don't worry that new people will take my place. There are enough good people to go around. I also don't feel that this ability is restricted to just a few people because it comes from God and His energy is limitless.

Do you find that being a psychic affects your family and social life? My son would always say that he could never do anything bad because "Mother would always know." Socially, sometimes when I'm out, people ask me to tell them what's going to happen to them. It's like being a doctor or lawyer and constantly being asked questions when you're not working. I guess people think psychics always work, and to some extent, we do.

If you make a dire prediction, are you upset about it afterward? Knowing about the JFK and Bobby Kennedy assassinations made me very unhappy. I didn't know much about them, but I predicted their deaths in my newspaper column before they happened. All the while I waited for the deaths to occur, I felt bad.

Have you ever tried to warn a famous person about a prediction of yours? I made a prediction on Canadian radio about Ted Kennedy's accident and then repeated it to him directly when I was in the Senate dining room. I told him he would be involved in an accident on or near water and that his companion would die but he would not be injured. He said to me, "I feel my family must have a curse on it."

Two weeks later, on July 19, 1969, Kennedy drove his car off a bridge, killing Mary Jo Kopechne and his presidential hopes.

How do you make your predictions? People give me their birthday but not the year. Sometimes I ask them to mention a color to get the juices flowing for me. I can then tell what is going to happen, whether I am talking to the person on the phone, on radio, on TV, or in person.

Who have you made your predictions for? I have worked with tens of thousands of "average" Americans; high government officials at all levels; royalty such as a Saudi princess; celebrities, including Howard Hughes when he was the world's richest man. I read for him and also did many readings for one of his accountants as well. I even read for one of the ten most wanted men in America before the FBI was looking for him!

What type of people do you help? I not only counsel individuals, I can do everything from forecasting the weather to solving murders. But finding lost people is not my thing. Still, I have assisted in more than two thousand murder investigations in several countries and have had many hits in this area.

How do you work with the police? Let's say the police are considering several suspects. I will have them put their photos down on a table and I turn them over, close my eyes, touch the photos with my fingertips, and meditate over them an hour or so each time. Sometimes I work with clothing. Touching the photo or the clothes usually tells me something about the crime—and sometimes even about the police officers.

Give an example of your success in this area. In one instance, not only did I tell the police who committed the murder from the photos they showed me but I told one of the policemen that when he got home, he would learn some shocking news about his father. When he returned, he was told his father had been flown to a hospital with a heart condition!

Are you good at weather predictions? Farmers call me all the time because I'm probably the best astrometeorologist in the world. My weather predictions are made as far as three years in advance and are extremely accurate. I can predict weather the same way I predict other things.

Have you done any ghost hunting? I have investigated and found many ghosts. I believe every house is haunted because every person who lived there leaves emotional footprints.

Once I found a house where chiropractic students were being bothered by the ghost of a medical doctor who was angry with the students for becoming chiropractors.

When did you come into national prominence? In 1966, I predicted in the newspapers the exact date of the great Chicago snowstorm of 1967. My husband was very unhappy during the storm, especially since the weather forecasts only called for four inches of snow ending by nighttime. "Look out the window and see what you started," he complained.

What is your background? I was born in a log cabin

on a farm in Tennessee. I came from a large family—I was the seventh of eleven children—that tilled the soil for a living.

My mother was half Cherokee Indian and could read the future in coffee grounds. She encouraged me, and as a child I felt that I knew too much. It was as if my whole head opened up. I knew everything that was going on with my older brothers and sisters.

Have you made successful predictions concerning your own personal life? In 1941 I met a man named Bill at an amusement park as I was going to a roller-coaster ride. Four months before that, I had written the name Bill on a slip of paper and put it under my pillow. I knew that would be the name of the most important man in my life, and he became my husband.

Do you believe children are psychic? Yes, many of us have unusual experiences when we are young, but our parents talk us out of them by telling us that these "visions" are just our imagination. Or when we "see things," they tell us we're daydreaming. Many extremely good psychics never develop, and when they grow up, they still have these experiences and are unable to handle the situation.

How did your own mother handle your being psychic? I was lucky that she was sympathetic, even though I sometimes embarrassed her. As a child, I saw astrological symbols for people and judged them on that. For example, I once called a very nice minister "a snake" because I saw the sign of Scorpio above his head.

How do you make your predictions? People say we make predictions, but that's false. We *receive* them. The sensitive intuitive brain transforms these waves into pictures, sounds, and symbols that the psychic verbalizes.

Can you give specific examples of how people can develop their ESP? I have taught workshops on this. I have my students place a personal object in a paper bag. Then each student selects an item and concentrates on getting psychic messages from the person the object belongs to.

In another exercise, students will draw a picture of an

object and then exchange the pictures with other students who try to tell something about the artist that way.

You're an ordained Baptist minister who spent seven years in the seminary. How does your faith in God fit in with your psychic abilities? There is nothing antireligious about psychic phenomena. Jesus himself performed miracles that could never be classified as regular occurrences. He healed people, could read people's minds, and communicated with the living after death. The Bible is built on a series of prophecies and mystical revelations.

RUTH MONTGOMERY

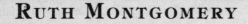

C/O G. P. PUTNAM & SONS
200 MADISON AVENUE
NEW YORK, NEW YORK 10016

*The first lady of the psychic world, her
fifteen books have sold millions of
copies and have been translated into
twenty-six languages.*

What do you do best? I think I was born to write.
Before I began producing books about psychic phenomena,
I had a newspaper career as a highly respected journalist.

When did you start writing? When I was eleven years
old, I secretly entered a writing contest intended for adults.
I left out the fact that I was a fifth grader and won first prize!

***What were some of your journalistic coups be-
fore you started writing about psychic matters?***
I hate to sound like I'm boasting . . .

Go ahead. All right then. I headed Eleanor Roosevelt's all-woman White House Press Conference Association and was the only woman permitted to cover FDR's funeral. I obtained the first exclusive interview with Juan Perón after he became president of Argentina. I was the only woman in the press entourage accompanying President Truman to Key West for his vacation in 1952 and, while there, flew over to cover the Battista Revolution in Cuba.

From inside sources that I developed there, I learned that Fidel Castro was a Communist. Seven years later, when Castro took over the country, Allen Dulles, director of the CIA, lamented, "If only we had known before that Castro was a Commie." But I had been writing this in my articles for some time.

What was your first headline story? In 1935, the *Detroit Times* assigned me to interview Doris Duke, heiress to the great tobacco fortune; she was called the wealthiest woman in the world. She has been in the papers a lot lately because of the suspicions surrounding her death. At that time she was honeymooning, and she had never granted an interview in her life. When I requested an interview from her, she slammed down the phone.

How did you get the interview? I waited outside her hotel suite and squatted beneath an enormous tray that a waiter from room service was carrying in to them. Doris was sitting there, bundled up in a full-length mink coat and galoshes, with massive curlers in her hair. I walked over to the table and identified myself. We shared a good laugh together, I got the interview and an eight-column front-page headline: "Doris Duke Gives First Interview Here."

What psychic stories of yours made the greatest splash? Of all the presidential campaigns I've covered and all the international dignitaries I've interviewed, no story ever received more reader response than the series I did on séances.

What was it called? "My Visit to the Spirit World." It was an eight-part series that ran in 1956 in hundreds of newspapers throughout the United States. My employers at INS, now known as United Press International, said they had never seen anything like it. Day after day, bundles of canvas bags of mail were forwarded to us by newspapers from all parts of the country.

How did you come to be interested in séances? I went to one out of curiosity. When the medium correctly identified my pet name for my deceased father, who wanted to talk to me, and gave other evidential material, I was intrigued. I then attended more séances with other mediums and spiritualist groups to gather material for the series.

What was the reaction to your stories from people you met? Everywhere I went, people began opening up and telling me story after story of their own psychic experiences. Equally bizarre experiences were told to me by everyone from generals and ambassadors to people like Mrs. William Faulkner and Mrs. Douglas MacArthur II.

How did you end up doing automatic writing? I became friends with Arthur Ford, a famous medium who convinced me to attempt automatic writing. To do this, I was supposed to meditate, then hold my pencil lightly on the paper and allow entities from the other side to write through my pencil. I was told to let whatever happened come through. In my case, *nothing* happened at first. But then, one day, a spirit friend, a man who calls himself Lily, came through, and he's been with me ever since.

Do you still do automatic writing? Yes, but I abandoned the pencil and paper technique in favor of the typewriter years ago. And I haven't changed to a computer.

You're best known not for your automatic writing but for your books. What are they about? I have written fifteen books, ten in the psychic field. They run the gamut from reincarnation to Atlantis to walk-ins to life after death to healers to extraterrestrials on this planet. I also discuss my own personal psychic journeys in *A Search for the Truth* and *Herald of the New Age*.

Of all that you've accomplished in your life, what has given you the most pleasure? My fan mail is full of letters that start out: "You have changed my life for the better," or "You have completely eradicated my fear of death." The reactions that I get on how my books have revolutionized people's lives and helped them to realize the continuity of life after death bring me great personal satisfaction.

Books by Some of the 100 Top Psychics

Frederick Baker and Jeannine Parvati Baker, *Conscious Conception: Elemental Journey Through the Labyrinth of Sexuality.* Monroe, Utah: Freestone Publishing, 1986.

Jeannine Parvati Baker, *Hygieia: A Woman's Herb.* Monroe, Utah: Freestone Publishing, 1995.

Jeannine Parvati Baker, *Prenatal Yoga and Natural Birth.* Monroe, Utah: Freestone Publishing, 1986.

Litany Burns, *Develop Your Child's Psychic Abilities.* New York: Pocket Books, 1989.

Litany Burns, *Develop Your Psychic Abilities and Get Them to Work for You in Your Daily Life.* New York: Pocket Books, 1987.

Arlene Dahl, *Beautyscope* (12 books). New York: Pocket Books, 1968–1996.

Arlene Dahl, *Lovescopes,* New York: Bobbs-Merrill, 1983.

Kenneth Dickkerson, *How to Win Games of Chance.* New York: Ballantine, 1992.

Ann Druffel with Armand Marcotte, *The Psychic and the Detective.* Norfolk, Virginia: Hampton Roads Publishing Co., 1995.

Jim and Pat Fregia, *Know Your Dreams, Know Yourself.* Berkeley, California: Celestial Arts, 1994.

Laeh Maggie Garfield, *Angels and Companions in Spirit.* Berkeley, California: Celestial Arts, 1995.

Linda Georgian, *Communicating with the Dead.* New York: Fireside, 1995.

Linda Georgian, *Your Guardian Angels: Use the Power of Angelic Messengers to Enrich and Empower Your Life.* New York: Fireside, 1994.

John Green, *Dakota Days.* New York: St. Martin's, 1989.

Karen Hamel-Noble, *Through These Your Hands with Mine.* Stillwater, Oklahoma: First Word Publishing, 1989.

John Harricharan, *Morning Has Been All Night Coming.* New York: Berkley Books, 1991.

John Harricharan, *When You Can Walk on Water, Take the Boat.* New York: Berkley Books, 1986.

Beverly Jaegers, *Beyond Palmistry.* New York: Berkley Books, 1992.

Beverly Jaegers, *Haunted House Investigation.* St. Louis, Missouri: Aries, 1990.

Beverly Jaegers, *Psychometry: The Science of Touch.* St. Louis, Missouri: Aries, 1979.

Beverly Jaegers, *Your Career Is in Your Hands.* New York: Berkley Books, 1995.

Kathleen Johnson, *Celestial Bodies.* New York: Pocket Books, 1987.

Kenny Kingston, *Guide to Health and Happiness.* Studio City, California: Windy Hill Publishing Co., 1984.

Kenny Kingston, as told to Valerie Porter, *I Still Talk To.* New York: Berkley Books, 1994.

Komar with Brad Steiger, *Life Without Pain.* New York: Berkley Books, 1981.

Dr. Gerri Leigh, *The Future Is in Your Hands.* New York: Dell, 1982.

Kurt Leland, *Menus for Impulsive Living.* New York: Doubleday, 1989.

Armand Marcotte and Ann Druffel, *Past Lives, Future Growth.* Norfolk, Virginia: Hampton Roads Publishing Co., 1993.

Patricia L. Mischell, *Beyond Positive Thinking: Mind-Power Techniques.* Cincinnati: Twin Lakes Publishing, 1993.

Ruth Montgomery, *Aliens Among Us.* New York: Fawcett, 1986.

Ruth Montgomery, *Born to Heal.* New York: Fawcett, 1986.

Ruth Montgomery, *Companions Along the Way to Tomorrow.* New York: Fawcett, 1986.

Ruth Montgomery, *Here and Hereafter.* New York: Fawcett, 1985.

Ruth Montgomery, *A Search for the Truth.* New York: Fawcett, 1985.

Ruth Montgomery, *Strangers Among Us.* New York: Fawcett, 1984.

Ruth Montgomery, *Threshold to Tomorrow.* New York: Fawcett, 1985.

Ruth Montgomery, *A World Before.* New York: Fawcett, 1985.

Ruth Montgomery, *A World Beyond.* New York: Fawcett, 1985.

Ruth Montgomery with Joanne Garland, *Herald of the New Age.* New York: Random House, 1988.

Nancy Myer and Steve Czetli, *Silent Witness: The True Story of a Psychic Detective.* New York: Birch Lane Press, 1993, St. Martin's, 1995.

Kathlyn Rhea, *Mind Sense.* Berkeley, California: Celestial Arts, 1988.

Shawn Robbins, as told to Milton Pierce, *Ahead of Myself.* Englewood Cliffs, New Jersey: Prentice-Hall, 1980.

Shawn Robbins with Ed Susman, *Prophecies for the End of Time.* New York: Avon, 1995.

Dayle Schear, *Dare to Be Different*. Nevada City, California: Blue Dolphin Publishing, 1992.

Dayle Schear, *The Psychic Within: True Psychic Stories*. Nevada City, California: Blue Dolphin Publishing, 1994.

Dayle Schear, *Tarot for Beginners*. Nevada City, California: Blue Dolphin Publishing, 1994.

Penelope Smith, *Animal Talk: Interspecies Telepathic Communication*. Point Reyes, California: Pegasus Publications, 1989.

Penelope Smith, *Animals. . . . Our Return to Wholeness*. Point Reyes, California: Pegasus Publications, 1993.

Shirlee Teabo, *Evolution of a Psychic*. Seattle, Washington: Tukwila Printing & Publishing, 1990.

Montague Ullman, Stanley Krippner, and Alan Vaughan, *Dream Telepathy*. Jefferson, North Carolina: McFarland, 1989.

Alan Vaughan, *Incredible Coincidence: The Baffling World of Synchronicity*. New York: Ballantine, 1989.

Joan Ruth Windsor, *Passages of Light: Profiles in Spirituality*. Williamsburg, Virginia: Celest Press, 1991.